QUEEN VICTORIA'S PRIVATE LIFE

Other books by E. E. P. Tisdall

MARIE FEDOROVNA:
Empress of Russia

ALEXANDRA:
Edward VII's Unpredictable Queen

QUEEN VICTORIA'S PRIVATE LIFE

1837-1901

E. E. P. TISDALL

The John Day Company

New York

FIRST AMERICAN EDITION 1962

© 1961 BY E. E. P. TISDALL

Library of Congress Catalogue
Card Number: 62-7339

Manufactured in the United States of America

Contents

Illustrations

PART ONE

Joseph and Eliza

I

'Our Little Vicky'

'THE Procession being formed, I replaced my crown (which I had taken off for a few minutes), took the Orb in my left hand and the Sceptre in my right, and thus *loaded* proceeded through the Abbey, which resounded with cheers.'

That Coronation self-portrait of Queen Victoria – *loaded* is strongly underlined – suggests in her a flippant rather than a reverent attitude on that tremendous day. True, the sacred Orb was indeed a cruel load for a tiny wrist. Its flashing mockery at her suffering must have stirred her indignation. The Queen's sudden desperate, angry appeal had shocked the dozing group around the throne.

'—What shall I do with this?'

It was the voice of a spoilt child: but somebody behind her had been equal to the occasion.

'—Hold on to it, Ma'am!' he advised in a firm but sympathetic tone.

The cool words had braced the Queen, averting any irregularity in the ancient ceremony, which, pursuing its endless way entirely unrehearsed, was sometimes a bewildered and angry adventure.

All through the dragging hours in the Abbey the shining eyes of Lord Melbourne, the Prime Minister, gazing obliquely upon her from beside the throne had offered her comfort. Afterwards the royal diary ran, 'my excellent Lord Melbourne, who stood very close to me during the whole ceremony, was completely overcome—' It was her most thrilling memory of Coronation Day, and the diary went on to reveal her joyful awareness of that unflagging precious look of possessive adoration which had sustained her.

With this hot June day of Crowning in 1838 the nineteen-year-old Queen Victoria was dedicated to her extraordinary reign of six decades, which carried her into the present century. It is a reign which divides into three clear-cut episodes: first, that of the Virgin Queen – one story contends that she once planned to pursue that lonely way through life; secondly, that of the wife of Prince Albert, the 'Uncrowned King', thirdly, that of the Widow of Windsor.

The third episode, the longest, and by far the most interesting, is that with which we are chiefly concerned. At last the Queen without Lord Melbourne or Prince Albert to control her was 'on her own hook' – to use an expressive slang phrase of her middle years, and the grim experience soon proved not only the stupendous strength of her personality and her true quality, but also set her drifting down some strange channels.

It was the human side of Queen Victoria – her faults, her frailties, her self-obsession, her obduracy, her sharp and scalding tongue, her arrogance, her laziness, her hopeless inconsistency and baffling eccentricities, all monstrously magnified by a volcanic force of character suddenly developed in widowhood, which made her a sovereign of heroic proportions. It was the dramatic side of her, in which she revelled with total disregard for the opinions of others, which in spite of her swept her to semi-divine glory in the very years when she was doing her best to make the monarchy highly unpopular.

Without the piquant sauce provided by this rich display of earthy humanity, her shrewdness and power of perception, her tremendous patriotism, her high sense of majesty and national custodianship, her genius for the office of Queenhood, could not by their merits alone have set her on her pinnacle. Her faults served to magnify the calibre of her greatness.

But before coming to the story of the royal widowhood, it is essential to recall episodes in the two earlier phases of Queen Victoria's reign: the days before and during her marriage. In the tempestuous pre-marital period, for instance, certain strains were emphasized in her character, which seemed to vanish after her union with Prince Albert, but reappeared with disconcerting force as soon as he died. Here lie the clues to the future.

· · · · ·

The nineteen-year-old Queen who was crowned on 28 June 1838 was not the same girl who had enchanted the nation in the months after her midnight accession in the previous summer. Then she was a fresh and magical novelty indeed, after the mad and bad old men who at last had vacated the Throne.

Thomas Creevey, the aged diarist, had first seen her on a fine August evening of 1837 when he had been feeding the ducks during his walk in St James's Park. A commotion outside the Palace had brought him running to the Palace railings. The little Queen was climbing into a barouche. Creevey noticed how tiny she looked. The Duchess of Kent followed, and the crowd eagerly identified the Queen's mother. But a third lady who took her place opposite the royal pair had the people guessing. A Cockney shouted out, 'It's the Nurse!' and a roar of laughter went up. The barouche passed slowly through the gates beside which Creevey stood. 'She looked even pretty with a most agreeable smile and the prettiest manner possible to us all without acting,' he entered in his diary that night.

The old man was still absorbed by his interest in the Queen a month later. 'Let me see what tidings I have for you of little Vic,' he wrote to a friend. He had gone over to Windsor with a party on a Saturday afternoon to see the Queen ride out with her company, and they waited by the Castle Gate, listening for the crash of arms from the guardhouse and the clatter of hoofbeats.

'On they came, at a smart pace, nearly twenty in number – the King of the Belgians, Vic and the Duchess of Kent in the first row, but the Boss King very gallantly held his horse in a little to let his Queen niece be first . . . as I stood with my hat off the Duchess was pleased to make me a very gracious bow. I was quite delighted with Vicky in every way. She looks infinitely better on horseback than in any other way; she was dressed so nicely too, and her manner *quite perfect*. I saw Melbourne in the group.'

Soon Charles Lamb, Lord Melbourne, would always be in the group and trotting familiarly beside the Sovereign – an absolutely novel occupation for a Prime Minister – while the redoubtable Duchess of Kent would have dropped out of the parade.

In October, Creevey was aware that Lord Melbourne had practically moved in at Windsor, and then followed the Queen to the Royal Pavilion at Brighton. He knew that every night Melbourne took the Queen's hand and led her in to dinner; but accounts of the goings-on at Court of an evening which reached Creevey were not impressive to a veteran of the Regency. They played letter games with printed letters and initials from a box, or put together map puzzles, and at half past ten the Queen went to bed. 'What an innocent Court, at all events!' exclaimed the diarist.

Melbourne was clearly envied by Creevey for his constant proximity to little Vicky. Perhaps some other enchanted outsiders were also jealous of the Prime Minister's luck. The leaders of H.M. Parliamentary Opposition in the House, if not envious, were certainly bewildered; for those proud Tory aristocrats and their ladies were being left quite out in the cold as far as royalty was concerned. That kind of attitude towards the Opposition had not been the custom in the previous reigns, shabby and disreputable affairs as they had been.

But as yet there was no breath of scandal or expression of doubt about the unique liaison between the Queen and her Prime Minister. Melbourne, who had certainly suffered some grim patches in his life, had struck lucky in his lonely maturity.

Haytor, the rising young artist, who was painting the Queen on her throne, had assured Creevey that Her Majesty decidedly possessed a mind of her own. Haytor had actually heard her disagree sharply with her uncle the King of the Belgians, to the surprise of that monarch who thought he knew everything. The diarist Creevey, of course, wanted to hear the artist's personal impression of little Vic, and was able to write to Miss Ord, 'he (Haytor), like everyone else, is quite in love with her, and he spoke most scientifically of the extraordinary character of her eye. He considers her as a truly great personage as to understanding.'

One charming characteristic of the girl Queen was noted by Fanny Kemble, the great actress, who was privileged to shake the royal hand in the royal box during a performance. The royal Hanoverian voices of both sexes were expected to be thick and ugly: Queen Victoria's was 'exquisite', in Miss Kemble's professional opinion – 'the enunciation as perfect as the intonation was melodious – it is impossible to hear a more excellent utterance than that of the Queen's English by the English Queen.'

Even before old Creevey died in the Spring of '38 there were jokes to be heard in high places about the Queen and the Prime Minister; but the jesters were professional wits not taken too seriously. Lady Grey wrote to him, 'I hope you are amused at the report of Lord Melbourne being likely to marry the Queen. For my part, I have no objection!' Yet, six months later, people were talking in no tone of light banter. Perhaps the talk was inspired and the flames fed by the great Tory families, who had been snubbed by the Court. In any case, with the widely reported developments at Windsor it was inevitable that the middle-aged bucks and jaded belles of the Regency would begin to raise their eyebrows, since they were given such a good excuse for doing so. Besides, little Vicky was no longer liked so well. She was said to be frighteningly headstrong, she was bold and brassy, too short and sharp, angry if she was crossed and did not take things seriously enough. Melbourne was giving her her head, or losing his touch on the reins. People were beginning to wonder where the little mare might bolt to in the end.

Lord Melbourne was the only male who entered the Queen's private sitting-room, and there he was alone with her for several hours each day. Some whispered that anybody trying the door would find it locked. Laughter sounded from inside. We know from the Queen's own diary that they discussed the Duchess of Kent in high merriment, deciding that 'Mama' was 'a liar, a hypocrite, a fool', who could never be trusted. The women in Melbourne's past were a popular subject for royal examination. Some *risqué* stories were enjoyed, and once they discussed the Holy Trinity, deciding that neither was theologically minded. Certainly, if the Queen had not been the Queen anything might have happened behind the closed door of the royal room.

Melbourne was a widower of fifty-eight years old, slim and youthful of figure, with a fine head of hair, twinkling eyes and sardonically mischievous lips. He might have successfully pretended to be in his forties. With women Melbourne was charming and most amusing. If he had not taken charge of the girl Queen somebody else would have had to do so: she had no private secretary. It would have been much more sinister if the Queen's mother or some male member of the royal Household had appeared as her mentor and guide.

The trouble was that the Prime Minister had fallen hopelessly in love with the Queen, and that she, needing him so much and finding him her only real friend at Court, could soon scarcely bear the hours when he was out of her sight. Besides being the only man she had ever known intimately, he was by instinct a professional charmer, and he was soon making no effort to hide his adoration.

If Melbourne was detained in Town by some personal or national business and did not enter her room at Windsor when expected, the Queen in tearful rage scribbled in her diary – 'He *ought* to be near me!' At Windsor, Melbourne was not allowed to sit at the table with the gentlemen after dinner. As the train of ladies following the Queen vanished through the door the Prime Minister swallowed a hasty glass of port and slipped out after them, followed by a battery of sardonic glances. Very slowly and almost imperceptibly Melbourne's tense anxiety to please the Queen chilled the warmth of her passion for him and destroyed her need for him.

But in May 1839 Melbourne still meant so much to the Queen that when a Governmental tempest forced him suddenly to present himself at Windsor and offer his resignation, she was terrified and desolated by the shock.

When Melbourne entered the room to say good-bye the Queen

ran to him and catching his hand clung to it, gazing desperately up at him.

'You must not forsake me!' she whispered between her sobs.

Melbourne, after hesitation, mumbled 'No' – although he knew that the excuse to meet her daily no longer existed, and that if she still sought him she must dangerously imperil her reputation. He then stood waiting to discuss the details of the hand-over of his Government; but the Queen tumbled into a chair and gave way to a storm of noisy weeping. Helpless and deeply distressed he crept away and returned several hours later.

Next, Sir Robert Peel, the accepted new Prime Minister, stiff, ponderous and shy, called at Windsor. The Queen awaited him in grim silence.

'Oh, how *different*, how dreadfully *different*,' she bemoaned as soon as she could escape from the unhappy interview and reach her diary.

But Sir Robert never did take up office. Shocked dismay and disappointment fell upon the Tories after twenty-four hours of anticipatory triumph. At his first interview he had mentioned the need for certain of the Queen's all-Whig Household to give place to Tory nominees. The Queen said nothing, but had Sir Robert known her better he would have felt her sharp hostility. As it was, he walked out with a sense of happy relief that the worst ordeal was over. While his carriage passed out of the Castle gate the Queen was writing to Melbourne: assuring him with vicious underlinings that his successor was a deceitful, deep, cunning person.

The following day Peel appeared again and suggested without embarrassment that the Queen might like to consider which of her Whig Ladies – it need not be all – should resign immediately. Suddenly he became aware that the Queen was glaring and goggling at him, her cheeks suffused with blood, as if seized by a brainstorm. There was a horrible pause.

'—*I will not give up one of my Ladies!*' said the Queen slowly and thickly.

Peel was terrified, panic-stricken. His nature was not equal to such scenes. He made up his mind at that moment and almost ran from the Castle.

As he saw it, he could not form a Government under such a Sovereign. To him, this trivial matter of a girl Queen storming at the prospect of living with some Tory Ladies was symptomatic of an issue of the deepest gravity – the Queen was a Whig, a Tory-hater, a monarch who thereby scorned the accepted Constitution of the Realm.

So the Tories were out: Melbourne's Whigs were summoned back to power by an ecstatic Queen. She danced about at Windsor like a happy fairy, unable to believe this wonderful thing had really happened.

That June at Ascot, when the Queen with Melbourne beside her, after driving along the Royal Mile, where the people cheered them, reached the royal Stand, she was loudly hissed by prominent ladies in Society: an ugly sound plainly audible above the feeble acclaims. A few minutes later she stepped to the front of the Balcony. From the enclosure a man of quality bellowed out 'MRS MELBOURNE!' and the fashionable throng murmured unpleasantly and glared up at her without sympathy.

Yet the reunion with Melbourne was not turning out wholly perfect even when they were alone. The Queen in fact no longer had her urgent need of him. For his part he, although the spell of the Queen still moved him, was growing jaded by his burdensome task. One day a friend assured him that he was handling the Queen most admirably. The Prime Minister regarded him with a wild look.

'—By God, I'm at it MORNING, NOON and NIGHT!' he shouted.

But Melbourne's day was almost done: a new figure hovered in the wings.

Prince Albert of Saxe-Coburg was the same age as his cousin Queen Victoria. He was the second son of Duke Ernst of Saxe-Coburg, whose sister had married the Duke of Kent and whose brother Leopold had married Princess Charlotte of Wales, only child of George IV, and after her death following a still-born childbirth had become first King of the Belgians. Prince Albert, brought up largely under the influence of his Uncle Leopold, had learnt when young that his probable destiny was to marry his Cousin Victoria. The prospect of a marriage to Cousin Albert had been suggested to Princess Victoria also when she was in her teens, but by no means so decisively.

The Queen had been just seventeen when Albert and his elder brother Ernst had arrived for a few weeks' stay at Kensington Palace. On that occasion she certainly had not fallen in love with her cousin. When the young Coburghers set out for home Victoria had wept, which she was rarely seen to do; but this was not caused by a girlish passion but because she saw herself condemned once more to the dreary solitudes of Kensington, and to her mother's naggings after an interlude of brightness. Not long afterwards her life became full of excitement and interest. She was a Queen – a wonderfully successful Queen whom everybody praised and adored – and she could do what she liked. She forgot about Albert of Saxe-Coburg. She forgot a certain little arrangement which Uncle Leopold had made with her, and to which she had light-heartedly agreed.

The Queen was disconcerted in the middle of '39 when Uncle Leopold gently reminded her of this understanding between them, pointing out that this was the year in which she had agreed to receive Cousin Albert in order to make her decision as to whether she did or did not wish him to marry her. Many Britons had long been of the opinion that King Leopold neglected his Belgians far too much in order to look after the affairs of the British, and the Queen now began to be of the same opinion. She bluntly wrote saying that she had changed her views about marriage: she did not want a husband for some time to come. King Leopold was unruffled. The thing to do was to wait until nature made her restless and discontented. He had always told Albert of Saxe-Coburg what he was to do, so he wrote and told him now that he would have to wait for several years as his Cousin Victoria was not yet willing to marry.

The effect of this announcement upon Albert startled his uncle. He answered that he was prepared to wait; but only with 'some certain assurance to go on'. It was, he declared, unfair that he should be made 'ridiculous'. The Queen, when informed of this, accepted her uncle's advice to receive Albert. She was annoyed; and perhaps moved by some feminine instinct she was also frightened.

Prince Albert set about his preparations with a heavy heart. He knew he had done the right thing by himself; but he did not look to the future with anything but dull dread. One Thursday night in October he stepped out of his carriage in the courtyard of Windsor Castle. The Queen had been awaiting his appearance at the top of the stairs to the royal apartments, and Melbourne standing close behind her knew that she was distinctly uneasy and short-tempered.

The bold blue eyes of the Queen surveyed the tall and handsome young German, who slowly and very coolly was ascending towards her. The brazen royal glance had flickered into softness and bewilderment before he reached the top and stood gazing down upon her in a solemn manner. The taut little fairy-like body of the Queen had gone limp. Did she sigh just audibly? The Prime Minister seems to have understood exactly what was happening. Had he had the privilege of reading the entry of that night in the royal diary, 'Albert is beautiful' the announcement would not have surprised him.

The Friday and Saturday which followed passed with the Queen in a happy daze. For once she was no trouble to anybody, and at some time during the family dinner on Sunday the Queen, who as usual had Melbourne on one side of her, gazed at him sternly.

'—I have a good deal changed my opinion as to marrying,' she informed him.

He received the news in amicable silence.

On Monday morning the Queen told the Prime Minister that she intended to marry Prince Albert. He knew that she was troubled as to how she ought to go about it, and he did not offer her advice.

Shortly after noon on Tuesday, Prince Albert obeyed an invitation to go to the Queen's room. If the huge supplicating blue eyes which scanned him touched his heart, the manner of the marriage proposal offered him was businesslike and unemotional. The Queen said that she would be very happy if he accepted her: she realized that he would be making a great 'sacrifice'. He, who so soon was to prove himself so accomplished in diplomacy, must have appreciated the neatness of her performance. He could without too much embarrassment to either of them have declined the responsibility; but as he stood there smiling gently in dutiful acquiescence the Queen perceived that she had secured herself her ideal husband, and instantly he was engulfed in the tight warm arms of an ecstatic little creature whose uninhibited passion demonstrated that she was a true Hanoverian.

Albert was the kindest of young men – '*an Angel*' – as the Queen informed the King of Belgium by letter that night. Secretly restrained in his feelings for his cousin as he almost certainly was, he was able to challenge the tempest of adoration which swept around him, until the hour of his homegoing to Germany, in a sturdy manner entirely satisfying to the girl who had chosen him.

The royal marriage took place on a cold wet February day of 1840 in the Chapel Royal, St James's. During the ceremony the spectators observed that the Queen constantly gazed upwards with adoring eyes at her tall bridegroom. He, set tightly in the unaccustomed glory of a British Field-Marshal's uniform, was apparently unconscious of the Queen's attention and came through with great coolness.

2

German Professor and Family

P RINCE ALBERT of Saxe-Coburg, the young husband of the
Queen, went by three nicknames among the British – 'the
Pauper Prince' – 'Lovely Albert' – 'the German Professor'.
Each of the names was meant unkindly, and none of the three was
inapt for the man.

For manly beauty, for grace of feature and figure, he was probably
the most perfect dandy in Britain in the year 1840. But he had no
money, looked a thorough foreigner, and was the 'German professor' because he never seemed at ease unless he was discussing
some learned, scientific, artistic or metaphysical problem.

Many of both sexes in those early days of the royal marriage
suffered a shock upon discovering that the husband of the Queen's
choice was upon acquaintance so cold and colourless. This was
especially the case with women, who approached the Prince with
curiosity and after a few minutes conversation were in no doubt that
as women they were of no interest to him. This was a sin they never
forgave and it lost him invaluable partisans in his setbacks with the
male aristocrats – 'the foxhunters', as he sardonically called them.

The plight of the Queen's husband was at the outset an unhappy
one: he was, as he may have foreseen, nothing but the royal stud
stallion and the sentimental plaything of the Queen in her spare
hours; and although it is evident that he treated his wife exactly as
she wanted to be treated, causing her thereby to trip about in a state
of joyous satisfaction, he must have felt utterly hopeless and
wretched.

'I am only the husband, not the master in the house—' Prince
Albert wrote, more in sorrow than in anger, to a German friend.

They had been married for three months and the Queen was known to be pregnant when one fine summer morning Prince Albert, who had never entered his wife's sitting-room when she was busy with Melbourne, walked in and saw that she was alone at the desk.

He regarded her earnestly and asked in a quiet tone why it was she never discussed affairs of public importance with him. Probably Prince Albert had been pushed into doing this by his Uncle Leopold, who had heard what a poor showing his nephew was making at the English Court. Baron Stockmar, his resident spy, kept him informed on such matters.

The Queen was startled at the sight of her husband. His manner arrested her even more than the impudence of his interruption. She coloured and would not meet his eyes as she murmured incoherent excuses. She was not angry and ended by hastily declaring that she would think it over. The Prince walked out, and something impelled the Queen to keep her word.

Lord Melbourne appeared a few minutes later, and the big blue eyes regarded him rather hopelessly as the Queen demanded what she was going to do about 'Albert'?

He laughed, and said that, of course, the Prince must be properly employed and that he would see to it. Prince Albert presently found himself invited to listen while his wife held meetings with her Ministers. He was not invited to attend at those intimate daily councils, sacred to the Prime Minister.

Nevertheless, Lord Melbourne henceforth adopted the Prince as his political pupil, and a kind of undergraduate and college tutor relationship grew between them. Melbourne was impressed by memorandums on foreign policy composed and submitted by the Prince, and other Ministers with a measure of genial condescension invited the young German to express an opinion upon this and that. They heard with surprise the replies which were sometimes offered them.

The Queen's husband was beginning to be noticed by men of mark if not by foxhunters and their ladies. Prince Albert began to feel his way into another sphere of activity. Perhaps the Queen's powers of resistance waned with her advancing pregnancy; for as the summer passed on it was observed that her much disliked German governess, Baroness Lezhen, was being used less and less as her personal secretary and that her husband was doing the work. When the news spread that the Baroness had decided to retire on pension the Prince was credited with the honours for this achievement.

It was the first stage in the development of that highly successful royal team, which became renowned through Europe in the mid-years of the century. At first the Queen was in the ascendant, although she sometimes caught herself listening when she should have been talking; then the pair were equal working partners; but within three years Albert was the one who led, while the Queen, living through a succession of pregnancies which lasted into the next decade, was happy to sit back in wondering admiration before an ever-increasing volume of brilliant works and achievements of statecraft performed by 'the Beloved One'.

When Melbourne and his Whigs had at last to go out in the Autumn of 1841, Prince Albert came into his own. Sir Robert Peel, the solemn Tory, was more to his taste. The Prince's friendship and understanding with the new Prime Minister, once scorned by the virgin Queen, set him firmly on his political feet and made him at the age of thirty the 'Uncrowned King', unfettered by the constitutional rules which bound his Sovereign wife.

Prince Albert got his opportunity right at the outset of the new order. Peel had only to appear and the old nightmare of the Queen's Whig Ladies reared up to threaten him. The Prince decided to tackle the problem for Peel. This was his first triumph, and it was completed without drama. The Prince thereby did a valuable service both to the State and to the Queen, and it was a pattern of things to come, when the key phrase would always be 'no fuss'. He chose his moment with care, and suggested to the Queen that he could arrange the lesser details of the essential change-over of Ladies without bothering her. He could finish the whole thing in a few talks with Sir Robert.

To this the Queen gratefully agreed, and settled down to await the birth of her second child.

Her first, the Princess Royal, had been born in November 1840. In the nursery she answered to the name of 'Pussy', and for the rest of her life to that of 'Vicky'. The first of the royal brood was destined to be the cleverest, and of the daughters the handsomest. She was to be the apple of her father's eye and in later days the most respected if not the best loved child of her mother.

Albert Edward, the Prince of Wales, came in the following October with the swansong of the Whig Ladies. From the first the Heir was seen by his father, not as a tiny boy child but as a being destined to follow a stern and unflinching path of duty to the end. In this son, Prince Albert would always be searching perplexedly for signs of himself and frequently finding with a cold-running of the blood the grim signs of Hanoverianism.

Alice was born in April 1843, and Alfred, the Duke of Edinburgh, in May 1844. The children were much attached to their Papa with the exception of Bertie the Prince of Wales, who soon began to have secret feelings on this subject which for many years he did not himself understand.

In the spring of '44 the Prince left the Queen's side for the first time to make a short stay with his brother Ernst in Coburg. There are phrases which occur in Albert's letters to his wife, which reveal a striking feature in their relationship.

In his first letter, written while waiting to embark at Dover and signed like the others 'your most devoted Albert' the sentence immediately preceding this restrained declaration illuminates almost comically the nature of his passivity.

'—You are now half a day nearer to seeing me again,' declares the Prince consolingly. 'By the time you get this letter, you will be a whole one – thirteen more, and *I am in your arms*.' (Author's italics.)

Nowhere in this letter or the subsequent ones does the husband assure his wife of his love, his adoration, his lonely yearning for her. But the first letter from Coburg does prove his tenderness of feeling for the little family group at home.

'—I enclose an auricula and a pansy, which I gathered at Rein-hardtsbrun. I have got toys for the children, and porcelain views for you. Farewell, my darling, and *fortify yourself with the thought of my speedy return.*' (Author's italics.)

That summer Prince Albert persuaded the Queen to let him reform the chaotic conditions reigning at Buckingham Palace and Windsor Castle. He had long endured with indignation and disgust the sight of liveried footmen who smoked in corners of the corridors or tottered with a blast of alcoholic breath into the royal apartments. He was tired of servants who excused themselves from tasks required of them because this or that was the duty of the Lord Stewards' Department, or the Lord Chamberlain's Department, or the Woods and Forests – or whichever department which did not employ them.

Which of the royal servants were selling food taken from the palace kitchens? Who was emptying the wine cellars? Who ordered goods in the Queen's name in London, that never reached the palace? Who in royal employ drew pay and stayed at home? What happened to the hundreds of part-used candles when daily fresh ones replaced them? Who could explain the huge monthly bills for domestic cleaning materials when the royal homes were uncommonly dirty?

The existing files of royal complaints, queries, inspectors' reports, repeated orders for repair of the same defects, the huge tradesmen's bills for regularly supplying unwanted replacements, justify the Prince's impatience. A vast cobweb, heavy with the dust of ages, had to be broken and swept out of the royal homes, and nobody wanted to help him do it.

When autumn came that year the homes of the Queen ran like well-oiled machines, the monthly bills had dropped by half, and Prince Albert was a tired man whose appearance in kitchen, cellar, scullery, pantry and housemaids' closet stirred dread, confusion and hatred.

But perhaps the economies inspired by Prince Albert stretched to more personal matters also. The Queen's annual dress bills covering these years are extant, and whereas in 1842 and during the previous years of her reign these approached £5,000 or slightly exceeded this figure, in 1843 her expenditure on dress was below £3,000. In 1844, the year of the palace reforms, the Queen spent only £1,965 8s 1d on her wardrobe. During the following three years the rise on this figure averages £4,000, accounted for in part by rising prices.

After some years of marriage the Queen, when discussing clothes or almost any other matter, seemed to find happiness in declaring, 'I have no Taste – I depend entirely on Him'. As a young Queen she had given great satisfaction by her attractive and sometimes rather dashing ensembles; but a new factor had entered into this matter. Prince Albert was always present when the traveller from Paris with his hats and bonnets was brought in to the Queen. Propped against the wall, his arms folded, the Prince gazed earnestly at his wife's head as each piece was set upon it. 'It won't do!' he muttered, and the article was replaced by another. At last an item, regarded by the ladies-in-waiting without excitement, was received in silence by the Prince, and the Queen after examining herself with curiosity in the mirror gave an order for it. He tackled the royal gowns as he tackled the hats, and took entire responsibility for the Queen's ensemble from head to foot.

The Prince's domestic achievements foreshadowed processes to be applied to the British Government, to the Army, to the Navy, to public life in general and to some extent to foreign sovereigns and peoples. Such brilliance, such astonishing versatility and cold persistence were beyond his wife; but she could recognize their worth.

This was the year in which the Queen wrote to her Uncle Leopold, telling him how popular with the people she and her husband were '—and this,' she added, 'because of our happy domestic life and the good example it presents'. It was true. The Press of the period bears witness to this in articles, pictures and more or less good-natured caricatures. Only two new publications, *Punch* and the *Comic Almanack*, with ambitions to amuse the upper-crust, poked rough fun at them. In that summer of 1844 when the palace reforms were underway, the Queen gave birth to another son, Alfred, the Duke of Edinburgh.

The Queen was spared the trials of childbearing in 1845 and in September the royal pair set out on a sentimental pilgrimage to Coburg, the scene of Albert's birth and childhood. They had to pass through Prussia, and the Prussians insisted upon making their passage a State occasion, ignoring their request to travel as private persons. On the rare occasions when the Queen's anger was really stirred into flame she used to prove too much even for her husband. This evidently was one of those, which must have been painful to Prince Albert. Nothing he could say would persuade the Queen to face duty cheerfully and behave in a royal manner, if Lord Cowley, our Ambassador in Paris, is to be believed.

He recorded in his diary '—All accounts from Germany are full of complaints of the Queen's behaviour upon her visit. Upon her arrival at Cologne she took offence at the *pas* having been given to the Archduke in preference to Prince Albert, the Queen of Prussia having taken the arm of the Archduke. The Queen in consequence refused to dine in public that day, and the King of Prussia put off the dinner which was to have consisted of one hundred and sixty guests. Her Majesty's conduct during the whole of her visit to Prussia was equally ungracious and offended everybody – and her meanness in money matters has made her the general theme of contempt and censure . . . Her Brittanic Majesty had better stay at home than have these displays of ill-temper and parsimony in a foreign land.'

The year 1846 was a sensational one for dwellers on the Isle of Wight, for the building of Osborne House began under the personal supervision of Prince Albert. Osborne is of immense importance in this story, because during the long years of widowhood which lay ahead of the Queen it was *Osborne* – not Balmoral, the place of refuge, nor Windsor, the grim Victorian stronghold – which was her spiritual home. The real Albert Memorial stands not in Hyde Park but on the banks of the Solent. Osborne House was His idea, He designed it, He watched its building, He decorated and furnished it inside, He laid out the splendid grounds and terraced gardens, planting and digging with his own hands. The Queen knew that more of her husband went into the creation of Osborne than into anything else he did in his life. Osborne was Albert's hobby, his escape valve from a life of feverish activity, full of disappointments, insults and frustrations and beset with burdensome problems, which for the sake of his adopted country he lifted from the shoulders of the incompetents around him.

To the Queen, Osborne was 'the dear paradise'. It was 'Albert's own creation – the impress of his dear hand stamped everywhere'.

Osborne might have been a nightmare even to a professional Victorian architect; but somehow this fantastic mass of pale stone crowning a balustraded terrace lined by statues with a great flight of stairs running to the glorious gardens and the sparkling waters beyond, held a mysterious harmony which puzzled the spectator who examined it piece by piece. Perhaps the exterior of Osborne succeeded because the royal builder had given it a soul.

The interior at Osborne was partly the Queen's creation, and the Beloved One had drawn out designs to meet her ideas. It was crowded with objects, the cheap and the priceless intermingled. There were pseudo-classical statues on revolving bases lining the hall – statues everywhere, guarding the bedroom passages, waiting in ambush round corners – there were garter blue alcoves surmounted by plaster shells and filled by family busts, ranks of imitation marble pillars, archways painted and figured, wallpapers and ornaments designed by Prince Albert and furniture covered in bright chintzes from his workshops. Landseers and Winterhalters shared the wall space with the Old Masters, with portraits and photographs of German relations and German views painted on cheap porcelain.

Everything envisaged by Prince Albert for his dream home on the Isle of Wight was achieved with astonishing speed on the £200,000 he had allotted for the task – the entire sum saved by his economies on the royal estates – and in due course, when the time was ripe, the painted wooden Swiss Cottage, two-storeyed and balconied all round, would arrive from Switzerland, and suddenly appear one morning a mile from the house to the delight of the royal children. Upstairs was to be the boys' workroom. The girls could cook and sew below. Their father would find time from the State boxes to keep an eye on both departments.

The Balmoral saga began in 1848, when they rented the old Deeside castle near Crathie, which they subsequently bought.

But before the Queen leased Balmoral there had been two further additions to the family: Princess Helena (Lenchen) born in 1846, and Princess Louise in the Spring of '48.

'—We have seen the Queen once since we have been in London,' writes her cousin Mary of Cambridge, later the mother of Queen Mary, in a letter of June 1848, 'she looked so young surrounded by her six dear little children. The baby Louise is the finest child I ever saw.'

At the old castle of Balmoral the inadequacy of the accommodation for the family, for the ladies and gentlemen, for the guests, the officials and the domestic staff seemed pleasing to the royal couple. The constant crush, the scrambling hotel manner of life, which endured for eight years, offered the communal discomforts of ordinary human beings. The Queen has recorded those simple, never-to-be-forgotten Highland episodes in her *Leaves from our Life in the Highlands* – those long trailing pony-back expeditions across the great hills, the fording of foaming floods with stalwart ghillies wading at the bridles and pipers playing ahead, the family picnics in the heather, the thrilling day-long stag 'drives', and the highlanders with their blazing pine torches, their whisky-wild dances, their solemn cairn-buildings, their pibrochs, their reels and laments. To the royal visitors this was a weird fairyland life as unrestful as the rainbow colours of the bewitching tartans in which they happily decked their persons and their furniture, their house-walls and their floors.

The royal team emerged well out of the Year of European Revolution, 1848, thanks largely to the cool wisdom of Prince Albert and his friendly alliance with the old Duke of Wellington. The sight of the Queen backed by her solemn husband, with a clutter of princes and princesses round her crinoline, would stir the common masses to enthusiasm at the turn of the half-century. But the Prince alone would not do. He frequently made official visits all over the land on his own, during which he was only too miserably aware of his unpopularity.

Publicly the Queen was little seen: she was too lazy, too self-centred, using the excuse of her parental duties and the State boxes to account for her secluded and pleasant life of domesticity. To the 'foxhunting' ladies, who took turns in serving her, she seemed a very *bourgeois* kind of person; but they thought her amiable and not very demanding.

Only once did the Queen's husband achieve unchallenged, resounding popularity – in 1851 with the Great Crystal Palace Exhibition. To compel the Britons of that day into sponsoring such a unique and monster entertainment, which drew the civilized world, was almost a miraculous feat. Only Prince Albert's courage, his drive, his quiet readiness to shoulder responsibility, his stubborn indifference to insult, his feverish energy and administrative genius made it possible.

The delirious opening day in that vast shining glass conservatory which enclosed giant elms, was an Albertian triumph, and the paeans of praise came even from excited 'foxhunters' as they flocked through its turnstiles.

The Queen, tearfully rejoicing at the long-delayed acceptance of the man she adored, wrote in her diary:

'This is one of the greatest and most glorious days of our lives, with which, to my pride and joy, the name of my dearly beloved Albert is for ever associated! – God bless my dearest Albert, God bless my dearest country, which has shown itself so great today.'

Prince Albert, assessing the popular outburst at its true value, agreed that, 'everything had been satisfactory'.

Three years later, in trying to negotiate with the Russians, and thereby stave off the Crimean War, since he knew Britain was entirely unprepared, he stirred the blackest suspicions among the

British. Nothing proves this so clearly as some crude verses of the time, which in the form of a best-selling broadside flooded the London streets. 'Lovely Albert', the Queen's husband, was it seemed a secret agent of the Russian Tsar!

'LOVELY ALBERT'
(an excerpt)

'—We'll send him home and make him groan,
Oh Al! you've played the deuce then;
The German lad has acted sad
And turned tail with the Russians.

'Last Monday night all in a fright
Al out of bed did tumble.
The German lad was raving mad,
How he did groan and grumble!

'He cried to Vic, "I've cut my stick:
To St Petersburg go right slap!"
When Vic 'tis said, jumped out of bed,
And wopped him with her nightcap.

'You jolly Turk, now go to work
And show the Bear your power.
It is rumoured over Britain's isle
That A—— is in the Tower!'

The last line spoke only the truth. With incredulity Prince Albert, who somehow found time to read every newspaper, realized one morning that these extraordinary Britons wanted to reward him for his endless hard work by locking him up in the Tower. Expectant crowds gathered at the Tower gates to watch Prince Albert brought in on a charge of High Treason. Among the eager spectators were those who declared that the Queen was coming to share a cell with him.

But the royal couple who entered the War under something of a cloud owing to public hysteria and calumny, emerged from the disastrous blunders and scandals of that tragic campaign more popular as a team than ever before; because their patriotism, their distressed concern for the neglected troops, their openly expressed anger and their efforts to right the situation had become common knowledge to the nation.

In the meanwhile two more additions had come to the royal family. Arthur, the Duke of Connaught, was born in 1850 and Leopold, the Duke of Albany, in 1853. There would be a four-year gap before Princess Beatrice, destined to a lifetime of patient and skilful companionship to her widowed mother, arrived to complete this family of four boys and five girls.

In the Autumn of 1853 the foundations of the new Balmoral Castle had been laid; and this was another of Prince Albert's monumental creations, but unlike Osborne it blended perfectly with the landscape and in conception was all of one piece. It inaugurated a more spacious era of royal life in the Highlands.

Among those natives of Crathie who watched this great mock-Gothic castle rising skywards must have been a big, red-whiskered, twenty-seven-year-old ghillie called John Brown. Two years previously the Queen, at the strong recommendation of her husband, had accepted him as her pony leader and outdoor personal attendant. Already the Queen was in the way of addressing her handsome young highlander with a freedom of conversation which could not have been allowed to an English groom, and Brown with a kind of brusquely humorous naïveté, which both startled and enchanted, was not slow to respond.

It would not be long before the sturdy figure of John Brown, with his glowing eyes, his flapping kilt and his astringent remarks, was for the Queen one of the more enthralling features of the Balmoral foreground when she sat wearily in England behind a pile of red Boxes and contemplated her longed-for annual holiday in the Highlands. But as yet John Brown's days of glory lay a decade ahead.

3

Twilight of Joseph and Eliza

A DISTINGUISHED French soldier has given us a picture of
Queen Victoria in her thirty-sixth year which is worth
recording. He was Marshal Canrobert, and the occasion was
the State Visit to France of the Queen and Prince Albert with Vicky
and Bertie, the Prince of Wales, in August 1855. She was the first
Sovereign to visit the *parvenu* Emperor, Napoleon III, and he, filled
with pride and delight, and basing his programme on his own
experiences at Windsor and London during the previous year, had
set out to make the French provide a dazzling display which would
greatly outdo this.

The Empress Eugenie – the first beauty of Europe – and her
delicious coterie of elegant but sadly inexperienced ladies-in-
waiting were commanded to array themselves exquisitely. This
was, perhaps, rather unfair to Queen Victoria.

Marshal Canrobert first watched the Queen stepping from a
newly-emblazoned carriage at St Cloud.

'—In spite of the great heat,' he recalls, 'she had on a massive bonnet of white silk with streamers behind and a tuft of marabou
feathers on top. Her face struck me as being amiable. Her dress was
white and flounced; but she had a mantle and a sunshade of crude
green which did not seem to go with the rest of her costume. When
she put her foot on the steps she lifted her skirt, which was very
short (in the English fashion, I was told) and I saw she had on small
slippers tied with black ribbons which were crossed round her
ankles. My attention was chiefly attracted by a voluminous object
which she carried on her arm; it was an enormous reticule – like

34

those of our grandmothers – made of white satin or silk, on which was embroidered a fat poodle in gold. The Queen seemed very small to me; but of a most amiable appearance; above all, in spite of the shocking toilette, I was struck by her dignified air.'

The Marshal sat beside the Queen at dinner, and if her manner deeply impressed him, her toilette once again gave him pain. The royal evening gown was white, and although a surprising display of bare bosom was not in itself objectionable to the Frenchman, he knew that this lowness was not in the fashion. '—She wore geranium flowers placed here, there and everywhere. She had plump hands with rings on every finger, and even on her thumbs; one of these contained a ruby of prodigious size and of a superb blood-red. She found it difficult to use her knife and fork with her hands thus laden like reliquaries, and even more difficult to take off and put on her gloves. On her head was a diamond aigrette, pushed well back; and she wore her hair in long loops which fell over her ears. Her eyes were beautiful; they were straightforward and intelligent, and she had a sweet expression which filled one with confidence. She had a good complexion; but her mouth rather spoilt her face which was otherwise pretty.'

Mary Bulteel, later the wife of Henry Ponsonby, the celebrated royal Private Secretary, was one of the Queen's Maids of Honour during the French visit, and she used to tell of the night when the Sovereigns visited the Gala Opera in Paris.

The Empress Eugenie was a breath-taking vision as she led her guests through the guarded corridors and the Queen was cruelly outshone. In French eyes the spectacle was almost pitiful. The Imperial Box now glowed with brilliance, and a gasp went up from the auditorium as the Empress in her glory appeared in the entrance. Then she hesitated. Either she did not know how to behave, or stage-fright vanquished her. An instant later the Queen slipped past the Empress and advanced until she touched the balustrade of the Imperial Box. There she stood alone and acknowledged the deafening acclaim with marvellous poise.

But the Queen, who dismayed the French by the style of her

gowns and bonnets and stirred their delight by her easy majesty, absorbed their attention in two other respects, as well. Her wide-eyed, naïve admiration for their Emperor and her undisguisedly flirtatious manner towards him were amusing; for he was usually given to making his conquests among the ladies of the demi-monde. The French were enchanted, besides, by the Queen's air of domesticity and her manner of possessive motherliness, as she floated along purposefully, in her swaying crinoline, while husband and children clung tightly in her wake. They called her '*La Bonne Mère de Famille*', and '*Le Home*' – a place looked upon by Parisians as a mere dormitory – became the new fashionable preoccupation of the budding Second Empire.

In the Emperor Napoleon III the Queen divined a compelling masculinity, a male attentiveness of a tense exciting quality, such as she can never have experienced with Albert. Did she fall in love with the Emperor? The Queen was no longer a girl, but a matron of thirty-six; her response to the virile male on this occasion should not go unnoticed, having regard to certain emotional developments in her later life.

'—A very extraordinary man – I might almost say a mysterious man,' wrote the Queen in a mood of breathless admiration, 'a great reliance on what he calls his star – wonderful self-control, even gentleness, with a power of fascination most sensibly felt, so full of respect and kind attention. I know few people whom I have felt more involuntarily inclined to confide in. I should not fear saying anything to him. I felt – I don't know how to express it – safe with him.'

During the French visit the French Emperor became aware of a fact concerning the British royal family, which was unknown either to the Queen or her husband. Bertie, the royal Heir, thirteen years old, was a secret malcontent in the family circle. The Emperor one afternoon drove the Prince of Wales into Paris in his private phaeton. Alone together for the first time the two got along famously. From the boy's talk it was easy to detect that he was being over-tutored and over-driven in every way. Suddenly, as they pounded along on the return journey the Prince of Wales spoke out with shocking abruptness.

'You have a nice country,' he announced. 'I should like to be *your son!*'

Bertie was the victim of his well-meaning and anxious father, whom already he feared and disliked; and every year the mother whom he had once thought of as a possible ally gave way more and more to Papa. The pair of them, Papa and Mr Gibbs, the smooth, fondling tutor, seemed sinister to him. The other royal brothers were too young to side with Bertie, and lacked in any case his strong and restless personality. Otherwise the family were, in fact, a closely-knit, happy one, and the Queen was thought by her intimates to be a successful and far from strict mother. Bertie stares sulkily out of all the family photographs of those days.

But the apparent oneness between the Queen and all her children but her eldest son seems in some way to have been inspired by the presence of Prince Albert; for when he came to die, as will be shown, a feeling of perceptible tension and unease grew between the royal children and their parent: a development which the Queen did not shrink from discussing with persons outside the family group.

The four royal daughters were devoted to their Papa, and so continued to the end. He indulged them in his slightly pompous, gently facetious way. Alice, on the threshold of her teens, teased him a little, and also disturbed him because he surmised that she might turn out rather bold and daring for a princess. But Vicky, the Princess Royal, was perfect. Of them all she was *his* child.

That September at Balmoral, Vicky, aged nearly fifteen, became engaged during a pony ride to Prince Frederick William of Prussia, eldest son of the Crown Prince. Prince Frederick William, with his budding whiskers and his officer-corps swagger, had already started his service with the Prussian Guards and looked toweringly mature beside his child fiancée. The affair had, of course, been arranged. Consternation had reigned for a few days at Balmoral because the Prussian guest who had arrived so purposefully was frozen in a fit of shyness and avoided the Princess Royal. But at last all was happily settled, and the Queen was sobbing and wailing in a prolonged spasm of distressful joy.

That afternoon to mark the engagement the first group photograph of the royal family at Balmoral was taken in the grounds, and this still exists in the royal Albums. A story concerning the Queen attaches to it.

Almost as soon as the happy pair had announced their engagement, which they did not do till they had exchanged their riding clothes for formal wear, a telegram was sent to G. W. Wilson, the celebrated Aberdeen photographer. In those days everyone who posed for a photograph had to control themselves during a long exposure. One restless person could ruin the group, and the Queen as yet had scarcely stopped shaking. Wilson, having completed his exposure, vanished into his tent, and reappeared somewhat unhappily. The family examined the picture and did not comment. Mama's face was blurred. Wilson, with the cool bluntness of a Scot, announced why it was amiss.

The Queen was first distressed, then indignant. It was agreed that another exposure must be taken, and the group rearranged itself. This time Wilson emerged from his tent with a better satisfied expression. A few days later the Queen and Prince Albert were out riding when they came upon Wilson with his camera directed upon the slopes of Lochnagar. Suddenly the photographer heard the voice of the Queen behind him. The tone was sepulchral.

'Good morning to you, Mr Wilson,' she said. '—No pictures spoilt today, I trust. How nice to have a sitter like Lochnagar, who can't fidget about!'

If the Queen had been secretly shocked by her husband's eager--ness to involve their immature eldest daughter in a dynastic marriage, she knew that the accomplishment of such a union fulfilled a dream that had long been with him. Prince Albert had decided that Prussia was the coming nation on the Continent, and that Europe ought to be led by Britain and the new Prussia acting in solid alliance. He was only moving into his middle thirties, so that he doubtless imagined for the closing decades of the century a grand partnership with

Britain slightly predominant and himself as the elderly arbiter of the nations. Having watched the young couple together since their engagement he came to feel joyfully that the marriage might really turn out a love match.

The marriage was not to take place for two years. The Queen had asserted herself about that. Vicky was not her best-loved daughter. She had been jealous of her for several years because of the almost passionate understanding between her and her father; but the Queen always respected character and she recognized this in Vicky.

In the meanwhile Prince Albert set himself to undertake the daring task of educating and training his chosen daughter for her tremendous destiny. The true nature of Vicky's future task in Prussia was only gradually revealed to her by her Papa as their studies progressed. She accepted all with pride and resolution. Unhappily, she was left too much with the impression that her duty was to Anglicize the Prussians; for Prince Albert, although disgusted and worn to a shadow by the British, had decided that that ungrateful nation had many superior institutions. Vicky's mother was also somewhat to blame over the problem of Anglicization. The Prince had suggested the benefits to be derived from some intimate and useful talks with the Queen, and her mother has proudly recorded some of the schooling she gave to the destined bride.

'Remember always – you will be at the same time your *husband's wife* and your *mother's daughter*. You will desire nothing else, but you will also forgo nothing which you owe to your husband and *your mother*.'

To act in all circumstances as a Prussian *hausfrau* and as the Princess Royal of Great Britain was an impossible assignment. It would probably have failed even had Prince Albert lived out his normal span. This beautiful, strong-minded child, although going to an excellent husband, was to be launched on a life of great unhappiness and frustration, and end her days with the ill-deserved reputation of being one of Europe's most dangerous women.

In 1857, the year in which Princess Beatrice was born, and in which the Queen appointed her husband *the Consort*, a new equerry joined Prince Albert at Windsor in February. He was Lt.-Colonel Henry Ponsonby of the Grenadier Guards, then in his early forties and a bachelor. For Henry Ponsonby this was the beginning of a long spell of royal service ending with twenty-five arduous years as Private Secretary to the widowed Queen and his death through overwork. He was a keen observer, and the ways of the Court being entirely strange to him, he saw everything from the outset with interest and curiosity. He made good use of his apprenticeship. Nobody came to understand the widowed Queen Victoria as he did, or saw as much of life at her extraordinary Court; but for years after his death the things he knew remained unrevealed.

The new equerry to the Prince posted a report to his mother from Windsor after his first weekend in Waiting. The Household dinner with Her Majesty, which he attended for the first time on the Sunday night had made its impression on him.

'The Dinner was rather awful. After dinner is very awful. We all stand jammed against a wall and our observations are necessarily few and of an uninteresting nature.' He had been pleased on the Sunday morning because the Queen had given him a smiling bow outside St George's Chapel. He had skated with the Prince of Wales before and after lunch – 'one of the nicest boys I ever saw' – and later Bertie had invited the party to his room, which was, 'very full of ship models'.

Henry Ponsonby regarded Prince Albert as humourless, ponderous and aloof, but took a liking to him. If he was precise, he was always affable and never impatient. The Prince had the bearing of an elder statesman, and although he was slightly younger than his new equerry was evidently regarded by Ponsonby as much older.

Only once during the periods of Waiting in his first year of office did Henry Ponsonby see the Queen's husband in a really human light. This was during the pheasant shooting, and it was an occasion upon which even the Prince's dignity collapsed into absurdity.

The Queen was always reminding Prince Albert not to shoot pheasants and game in general in the vicinity of Frogmore House, as the aged Duchess of Kent, with whom she was now on affectionate terms, strongly objected to this on the grounds of cruelty.

One day the Prince could not resist leading his party of guns towards Frogmore, and they started shooting. Pheasants were dropping right, left and centre when the Duchess of Kent on her way to visit the Castle was seen approaching in her open carriage.

Prince Albert was afraid of his mother-in-law. With a stern but panic-stricken look he ordered his party to squat behind some palings and joined them himself. The cover was poor, and the Duchess when rounding a bend in the road gazed in icy silence upon the Prince and his dozen gunmen. Upon reaching the Castle the old lady had the shocked appearance of one who had seen a ghost, and when questioned by her daughter told the Queen in a quivering voice that she had been 'inexpressibly surprised' at the sight she had had the misfortune to witness.

The Princess Royal was to be married in January 1858, but in September '57, when Prince Frederick William was the guest of the family, a shocking storm blew up. The Queen had assumed as a matter of course that the Wedding would take place at the Chapel Royal, St James's. Suddenly, the Prussians announced that their royal princes were by custom always married at home.

To Prince Albert, set upon achieving the Prussian match at any reasonable cost, his wife's threat to wreck it must have seemed like the old nightmare of the Whig Ladies. He was dismayed, but supposed he would have to settle it somehow to the Queen's satisfaction. But this time the Queen did not want his help.

'The Queen never could consent to it, for both public and private reasons,' she wrote to Berlin. 'The assumption of its being *too much* for a Prince Royal of Prussia to come over to marry the Princess Royal of Great Britain is too absurd, to say the least. It is not every day that one marries the daughter of the Queen of England. The question must be considered as settled and closed.' After the receipt of that heroic letter, *it was settled and closed:* the Wedding was held in London.

Prince Albert was never the same after the departure of Vicky.

Whether inside the family circle or out of it, he seems to have been only at one with this child. His brother Ernst of Saxe-Coburg already knew that Albert's health was breaking under the strain; but this fact now began to become visible to others, although the Queen appeared to ignore the signs and did naught to restrain her husband's immense labours.

One who was in favour with the royal couple was Lord Clarendon. While Foreign Minister he had come much in contact with Prince Albert, and although he was out of office in the late fifties he was a welcome visitor at Windsor, and was consulted on all kinds of matters. It is Clarendon who reveals that in Society they were nicknamed *Joseph and Eliza*.

Lord Clarendon frequently uses the nicknames in his letters. 'I was sent for by Joseph – Eliza dropped in,' is a typical sentence indicative of his faintly ironic attitude towards them. After a visit to Osborne he tells his friend the Duchess of Manchester, 'One must be up *very early* to tell this worthy family anything they don't know already'. The Queen, apparently, had informed him of certain scandalous details concerning a lady in Society, and in her turn had expected him to disclose certain facts supposed to be known to him about some gentleman in whom she was interested; but in this he had disappointed her.

Clarendon shows that in the fifties 'starchiness' was much less a characteristic of *Eliza* than it was of *Joseph*.

In a letter to the Duchess of Manchester (7 August '59), he describes the Queen at Windsor mimicking her Mistress of the Robes, who was a loquacious Gladstone enthusiast. The Duchess of Sutherland was an irritating woman on several counts, but to enthuse about Mr Gladstone was a thing incomprehensible to the Queen even in those days. Clarendon had just returned from being a guest at Windsor when he wrote, and he says that, 'nothing could exceed the Queen's kindness – if she had been my sister it could not have been greater'.

Sixteen-year-old Princess Alice was the first of the royal daughters to make her mark on the male element at Court. Vicky had been

bespoke so young that she had slipped away to Prussia almost
unnoticed. Besides, there was liveliness in Alice. She was not a
thinker. Whoever had the choosing of her wardrobe it can scarcely
have been the Queen, for in the family photographs the youthful
figure of Alice under big summer hats or piquant winter bonnets
stands out with refreshing allure. The graceful Princess had a will of
her own, like the Prince of Wales, but unlike him she loved her
parents and cheerfully ignored them in case of disagreement. Lord
Clarendon surmised that the parents were going to find 'that damsel
troublesome'. Probably Prince Albert decoded that a rather special
husband was required for Alice, as in the next few years he was
unable to find her a suitor.

In November, Lord Clarendon, whose contacts were wide, was
warned by a lady at the Prussian Court that something ought to be
done to stop the Queen pestering Vicky and giving her all kinds of
instructions. The Prussians were growing angry and suspicious, her
husband was upset and the Princess herself, torn between two
allegiances, was in distress. The Prussian lady expressed the opinion
that 'the Queen is really insane about her maternal authority', and
Clarendon believed his correspondent, although he thought
tyrannic a more apt description of her behaviour. But he could not
see himself approaching the Queen about this, because his knowledge
of her made him sure his interference would only make her worse.
The affair had taken on an added seriousness since the birth of
Vicky's son (later the last German Kaiser); for the Prussians now
considered her more than ever their property, especially as the old
King might die at any time and she would be the Crown Princess.

A break between the Queen and her daughter was thought
likely, and even hoped for in both countries; but this would never
come, and the dominion, or the alleged dominion, of Queen
Victoria over the Princess Royal was destined to be an explosive
element in Anglo-German politics until the last years of the century.

The first day of 1860 came, and a new decade opened. The sands
were running out for *Joseph* and *Eliza*, and the strange idyll was
almost spent. She was cheerfully content conducting the more or less

even flow of their family life. In State affairs it was enough for her to be inquisitive and appreciative of the works of the master. They carried their forty years very differently: she, smooth-cheeked and almost attractively buxom; he, paternal or avuncular beside her, a coarsening, flaccid elder with dead eyes.

Yet dismal as he felt and nearly spent, *Joseph* was ready to rejoice with *Eliza* when news came from Berlin in July that Vicky had given them a granddaughter. A few words in his congratulatory letter to the beloved daughter are worth noting, because these show his human side and thereby broaden the family picture. '—Little girls are much prettier than boys,' he informs Vicky. 'I advise her (his granddaughter) to model herself on Aunt Beatrice (b. 1857). That excellent lady has not now a minute to spare. "I have no time," she says if asked for anything. "I must write letters to my niece".'

In the autumn of 1860 when they were at Balmoral they embarked at Prince Albert's suggestion, on the first of the 'Great Expeditions', which the Queen has minutely chronicled with such gusto. A tragic undertone seems to run through this simple story. It is filled with a nostalgic melancholy, as if one half of the Queen somehow knew as she recorded them that there was a sense of finality about these expeditions.

Lady Augusta Bruce recalls seeing the royal couple in Scotland that September when the family were staying at Cramond *en route* for a shopping expedition in Edinburgh.

'It was very sweet on Sunday,' she writes, 'to see the Queen trot to Church through the grounds and the little gate in the churchyard near the stables arm-in-arm with the Prince.'

Henry Ponsonby was in Waiting during that last family Christmas at Windsor, and he tells of an evening early in the New Year, when it became known that he was engaged to Mary Bulteel, a Maid-of-Honour, to whom the Queen had been showing much favour. Now Ponsonby was to have his first experience of the royal possessiveness: that frightening quality which in the years ahead was so often to make his life a burden. Many years hence, Ponsonby's son would find himself involved in an almost exactly similar matrimonial situation and would stir much more stubborn indignation in the ageing Queen.

All through the evening after the engagement had become common talk, Henry Ponsonby was aware that the Queen was examining him with an unfriendly eye. Just as the family were departing to bed she called out to him rather brusquely and he hurried to her.

'I highly approve of your choice,' she said, 'but you are taking from me the best of my Household! Goodnight, Colonel Ponsonby.'

She had smiled bleakly; and in later years he came to realize she had forgiven him his offence surprisingly quickly. When he and Mary Bulteel were married a few months later the Queen invited them to rent one of her houses in the cloisters at Windsor.

Henry Ponsonby's bride was the niece of General Charles Grey, the Private Secretary of Prince Albert. General Grey was soon destined to take on the same duty for the widowed Queen, and from the time of his niece's marriage to Henry the friendship of Uncle Charles not only forwarded his nephew-in-law's career in the Household, but taught him much about the unique craft which one day he would pursue in his uncle's footsteps.

Late one cold February night in 1861 the Queen and her husband were driven swiftly over the frozen roads to Frogmore House. The Duchess of Kent was at last dying of the cancer which for months had made her life a misery. Nobody had thought the Queen excessively fond of her seventy-four-year-old mother. But when the body of the Duchess lay lifeless on the bed, all in the death chamber, even Prince Albert stood horrified watching the excess of violent grief displayed by the Queen at the bedside. She scribbled in her journal of 'the *weeping* which day after day is my welcome friend,' and added with pride, 'the approval of the manner in which I have shown my grief, is quite wonderful'.

In fact, the whisper had gone out from Windsor that the mind of the Queen was unhinged; and soon Prince Albert was hearing of reports from abroad which said that at last the Queen of England was going the way of her insane grandfather. Distressed both for his wife and because of the political complications which might follow such stories, he, who was in greater need of the physicians than she, interrupted his feverish labours to broadcast letters across the Continent denying the sinister rumours. With her his efforts to re-establish a life of normal behaviour did not seem to prevail. Only when she was ready did she resume the comfortable family routine.

Some surmised that the Queen's collapse, her wild declarations that her mother's death was 'the sorrow of her life', her most 'dreadful hour', came from remorse at the way in which she had earlier treated the Duchess – but did the shadowy lamp-lit death scene at Frogmore fill the Queen with a horrible, inexplicable dread of the fathomless future? Was she more worried about the condition of dearest Albert than she admitted to herself? Was she experiencing a kind of unconscious presentiment of a more terrifying deathbed at Windsor before this year was out?

A result of the Duchess of Kent's death was that her Lady-in-Waiting, Lady Augusta Bruce, was invited to become *Resident* Woman of the Bedchamber to the Queen. The idea of creating this, till then, unheard of post almost certainly stemmed from Prince Albert with the object of placing his wife under the control of a personality likely to be of benefit to her. Lady Augusta, then in her early thirties, and already well-acquainted with the ways of the family, accepted the post. Thereby, she became a kind of permanent *lady companion* to the Queen. That Lady Augusta did not from the hour of her entering the royal service in this guise stir up more jealousy and suspicion than was actually the case was a tribute to her own attractive nature.

One thing Lady Augusta quickly discovered with some dismay was that the Queen by no means shared her own horror of cold and wet weather. The first autumn at Balmoral had its trials for the *Resident* Woman of the Bedchamber. When rain splashed against the window and the wind howled round the turrets, a royal summons would come to Lady Augusta as she huddled over her sitting-room fire. Her Majesty was going out riding taking a picnic basket: the rain would surely stop soon or considerably abate.

Incredulous and shuddering the royal companion would pull on one thick gown over another and bundle herself with petticoats, oblivious of the mirth aroused by her bulging inelegance. And so she would ride away after the Queen with a happy smile. Once the Queen had started out nothing would drive her home until the appointed hour. She would even seat herself on wet grass on a storm-swept crest and order the luncheon basket to be opened. 'H.M. quite accepts the idea of sitting for hours perishing on a pony going at a foot's pace and coming home frozen!' complains Lady Augusta to her younger sister.

The royal family, both the mother and her children, stood on the threshold of a tremendous change, and it may be useful as this crisis approaches in their lives to review the Queen's sons and daughters as they were at that time.

Vicky, the Princess Royal, was twenty-one and had become Crown Princess of Prussia. She had one son and one daughter.

Bertie, the Prince of Wales, was almost twenty. He had done a spell at Edinburgh University and had passed from Oxford to Cambridge. Neither the quality of his work at these establishments nor his general behaviour had pleased his father, to whom in his mother's hearing he had sometimes addressed himself with cold insolence. The irresponsible conduct of the royal undergraduate troubled Prince Albert, who suspected that the heir was an incorrigible idler with no higher feelings, and interested only in amusement and freedom. That September, Bertie, when visiting Germany, had, through the contrivance of his sister Vicky, met the lovely Princess Alexandra of Denmark. His enthusiasm for the young Danish Princess, whose qualities Vicky was energetically sponsoring to her parents, raised hopes in the Queen and Prince Albert. Marriage might bring a great change in their eldest son; but nothing was as yet arranged.

Eighteen-year-old Alice performed her allotted task as monitoress of the brothers and sisters at home with a sprightly irresponsibility, always satisfying to the youngsters and usually passing muster with her parents.

Alfred, the Duke of Edinburgh, was seventeen and a midshipman in the Royal Navy. Already he knew that his destiny was to succeed his childless Uncle Ernst as Duke of Saxe-Coburg. A self-centred, talkative boy, Alfred was the least liked among the royal children by outsiders.

Helena and Louise were pretty, rather earnest girls of fifteen and thirteen respectively, who appeared to the world as sisters in close alliance.

Arthur, the Duke of Connaught, was a lively eleven-year-old, determined to be a guardsman, who took good care of his weakling brother Leopold, the Duke of Albany, aged eight. This guardianship of Leopold was very necessary. He was a haemophiliac, whom some doctors predicted would never reach manhood.

Golden-haired Princess Beatrice, a devastating and observant child given to solemn and ungrammatical remarks, was at the age of four much left on her own.

It was unfortunate that the Queen should have been able to trace the beginning of her husband's fatal illness to 24 November, a raw cold Monday, when he arrived at Cambridge. He was far from well and would have been better to stay indoors, but he had arranged to interview the University authorities in the hopes of extricating the Prince of Wales from some trouble in which he had involved himself.

He returned to Windsor in a feverish and troubled state. To the Queen he hardly spoke, and in the days which followed she complained in her journal that he was 'irritable and trying'. This was a most unusual entry; yet at that time she was plainly indignant rather than worried, and especially so when he declined to take the traditional daily walk with her.

Never before had Ministers of the Crown in search of the Prince been received by him in a dressing-gown and slippers. He never came out of his room. This was the period when the famous *Trent* crisis came to a head, and Lord Palmerston arrived at Windsor with his ferocious ultimatum to the Northern States of the Union, which since it was sure to be refused would bring Britain into the American

Civil War on the side of the Southern slave-owners. This was so unthinkable that the sick Prince staggered to his table and like one in a nightmare scrawled a brilliant dispatch which satisfied the honour of both parties and saved the peace.

On 4 December the Household heard that the Prince had collapsed on the couch in his room, declaring that he could work no longer. 'It's too much,' he muttered to the Queen. 'Too much – you must speak to the Ministers!' He had abandoned his desk for ever. He had abandoned his wife, his children, everything. It seemed to the puzzled doctors in the next few days that he was making no effort to control his illness. A second bed was brought into the room and placed beside his own, and they changed him from bed to bed to ease his delirious restlessness. At last the Queen admitted to herself that she was frightened. He had never spoken to her as on that day he roughly told her to 'see the Ministers'. His 'strange, wild look' had driven her away. 'I went to my room,' she wrote, 'and I thought that my heart would break.'

If the doctors were puzzled they did not admit this to the Queen. They told her that the sickness was gastric fever, which must rise to a severe crisis before an improvement came to the patient. The Household, watching the cheerful aspect of the Queen as the days went by, allowed this to lull their own fears of the extreme gravity of the hour.

On the morning of the 14th the Queen, who had been assured when she rose that the patient had awakened refreshed, came in a dressing-gown into the sickroom. Perhaps the Prince really had looked better upon first opening his eyes, for it was the doctors who had sent the message, and some dire change had occurred in him as the Queen passed from her room to his.

When she approached the bed one look at him was enough for her. She was terrified. Dazed, in horror and incredulity and with streaming eyes, she fled from the appalling spectacle to the corridor.

That night as the Castle clock struck a quarter to eleven Prince Albert the Consort died in the dim sickroom, with his wife, his elder children and the intimate Household kneeling around him.

The moment of death had not taken the Queen by surprise.
Called to the sickroom she had obeyed the summons in the manner
of a prisoner going to execution. Upon entering and finding the
others already gathered she had cried out, 'This is Death! – I know
It!'

When the body lay lifeless, she fell upon it, talking to it, appealing
to it with a flood of loving names. They half carried, half dragged
her to a sofa where she clutched the children to her one by one. She
started up, calling the Ladies and Gentlemen and the doctors
around her, and groping at their hands screamed, 'You will not
desert me! You will not desert me!' Then swiftly she was gone,
leaving them in a state of dismay.

Mrs Macdonald, an old servant, has described what followed, and
the simple words read like an epilogue to the tragic close of this first
great episode in the Queen's life.

'—It was an awful time – an awful time. I shall never forget it.
After the Prince was dead, the Queen ran through the ante-room
where I was waiting. She seemed wild. She went straight up to the
nursery and took Baby Beatrice out of bed, but she did not wake her.
That's so like the Queen. Orders were given at once for the removal
of the Court to Osborne. All the servants were sent off in haste. It
was thought necessary to get the Queen away as soon as possible.
It seemed as though her grief would kill her. She did not cry – and
they said that when she once got into the Prince's room no one
seemed able to persuade her to leave it. When the Queen did cry she
cried for days. It was heart-breaking to hear her.'

PART TWO

Eliza the Widow

4

Shades in a Black and Brown Court I

BRITAIN was shocked, horrified, by the sudden death of the Prince Consort at the age of forty-two. Millions had grown to understand what this strange solemn man had meant to the Queen: by 1861 they were also aware that he had been their real sovereign for years and that he had served them as no King, and few statesmen had done for a century, at least.

It was, indeed, as old Mrs Macdonald had said, a terrible time for those with the stricken Queen inside Osborne House. Only two people had admittance to her for several weeks: Princess Alice and Lady Augusta Bruce. Alice, who now appeared in her true colours and was much praised for her calm demeanour, was the link between her mother and the despairing, sometimes plainly indignant, General Grey. Day by day the Private Secretary watched his tables piling up with neglected State documents. Princess Alice took some to her mother, and after reading them aloud in the room of mourning told her to sign them. Papers of lesser importance the Princess could not be persuaded to carry to the Queen, and the Private Secretary was blamed for the confusion and dismay in Whitehall.

Lady Augusta in her role as 'guardian', moved by pity and loyalty, assumed an almost sinister role at Osborne. The atmosphere was macabre. The Queen was heard wailing and moaning by people passing in the corridors. Members of the Court wandering about in idleness fostered once more the stories that the Queen had gone mad, which spread through the country.

When a Privy Council had to take place the Queen declared that she 'was no longer concerned with earthly things'. Alice persuaded her to sit in a darkened empty room adjoining the Council chamber

with the door ajar and listen to the debate. The members, aware of
the hidden presence of the Queen, shouted in nervous voices as if
addressing a deaf person.

It was during those weeks that the Queen gave certain orders,
which held good until the day of her death. A photograph of the
corpse of Prince Albert lying on his death bed, surmounted by an
evergreen wreath, was to be hung a foot above the pillow on the
unoccupied side of every bed in which the Queen would ever sleep.
A servant was nightly to place a clean nightshirt on her husband's
side of the bed and a can of hot water in his basin. Some say that the
Queen, years after his death, was sometimes found clutching the
Prince's nightshirt to her with childlike fervour when they came to
wake her.

Photographers were to be called to Osborne, Windsor, Buckingham Palace and Balmoral to take photographs at all angles of the
Prince's rooms. In these apartments no object was to be shifted
from its position on the night when the Prince died. All the rooms
were overflowing with articles of every description, and the Queen
– far from being insane – foresaw that only a servant who was
supplied with the photographs would be able to dust each object and
replace it as before. In future days the cleaner of the Prince's apartments would hold an honoured place in the servants hall.

She was living on a more than earthly plane, and the problem for
the people she was supposed to be ruling was how to bring their
Sovereign back to the gritty soil. 'I lived only through him, the
Heavenly Angel . . . my only wish is to join him soon . . . I try to
comfort myself by knowing that he is always near me, although
invisible.' These words, written to her old friend the Queen of
Prussia five months after her husband's death (26 May 1861), are
followed by a seemingly somewhat irrelevant sentence, which is of
considerable interest in view of subsequent developments in her life.
'My nature is too passionate, my emotions too fervent, and I am a
person who has to cling to *someone* in order to find peace and comfort.' (Italics here are the authors.)

Soon after the dreadful event she had pictured herself in a letter to

her Uncle Leopold of Belgium as going when in trouble to the bed
where He had died and praying on her knees 'to be guided by my
darling to do as he would wish', and how a calm would come over
her, knowing her anguish was 'seen and heard'. There followed a
declaration notable not only in its relation to future events, but also
because of the way it conflicts with her passionate words to the
Queen of Prussia about that *someone* to whom she must 'cling'.

'I am *also determined* that *no one* person, may *he* be ever so good,
ever so devoted among my servants – is to lead, or guide or dictate
to *me*. I know how *he* would disapprove.'

The first news of the Queen after the arrival at Osborne came
naturally from Lady Augusta Bruce, who wrote to her sister:

'I cannot tell you what it is like to be here, to watch day by day
the progress of this agony. The whole house seems like Pompeii.
Life suddenly seems extinguished. Someone who came down on
business from Windsor said, "You are all so thin, there are such
lines of care on every face". Her grief, so touching, at times there are
terrible outbursts. Princess Alice is quite wonderful. What it is
given her to do and say you cannot believe.'

A fortnight later the situation had scarcely changed. 'They would
never have believed, no one could, how She is so totally heart-
broken, so daily feeling more and more Her desolation and misery.
The Queen feels very weak, and growingly so, but is not ill . . .
Darling, I do not agree with you that sons are easier than daughters
to bring up!'

This is a reference to the problem of the Prince of Wales. Bertie
had scarcely seen his mother since he knelt with her beside the deathbed. It was not his fault. Each time he had entered the Queen's room
at Osborne she had grown agitated, glaring at him with a kind of
suppressed fury, followed by a spasm of terrifying grief when he left
her. 'It quite irritates me to have him in the room,' she had gasped
in explanation after one of these bouts. To the shocked hearers her
words, cruel as these were, sounded mild compared to the viru-
lence of her behaviour in her son's presence. The Queen had decided
that Bertie had caused his father's death. By his behaviour the

wretched boy had taxed that tired noble heart till it broke. Lord
Clarendon had become aware of this as early as 24 January. He had
been told of it by no less an authority than the King of the Belgians,
who had come over to be with his sorrowing niece, but at that
moment was ill in London.

'—The only news he told me was disagreeable enough viz that
the relations between the Queen: & The P: of W: are as bad as ever,
if not worse, and that all his efforts to improve them had been fruit-
less – it seems to be an antipathy that is incurable . . . the Queen's
conduct in this matter is hardly sane . . . Leopold said expressly that
she was in a *healthy state of mind*.'

Lord Palmerston also knew a great deal about the Queen's attitude
towards her eldest son. He goes even further than Clarendon, and
speaks of her 'unconquerable aversion for the Prince of Wales'.
Clarendon, writing again a few days after his first mention of the
affair, which he foresees if it goes on must be a grave problem in the
State, has heard of the temporary solution which has been found for
it. '—Under all the circumstances how strange it is,' he reflects, 'that
She shd: get rid of the P: of W:! it's monomania . . .' The Prince's
projected tour with his tutor to the Middle East planned for the
Spring of '62 had been cancelled on his father's death, but now in
order to part mother and son it was hastily rearranged and put
forward to 22 February.

By 8 February the Queen was beginning to be seen a little about
the house and garden. Lady Augusta reports on that day, 'the Queen
sleeps more or less well. She weeps very much and that exhausts.
She now rises before breakfast, but has it in Her room . . . She has
seen Lords Clarendon, Granville, Russell, Palmerston, the latter
wept bitterly.'

It was the first meeting with outsiders and 'Pam', that doughty
political adventurer whose defiant scrapes had so often exasperated
Prince Albert, was completely reduced by the piteous aspect of the
royal widow. Clarendon talks of 'the Queen going into every detail
of the illness, his appearance after death, etc., etc.: which throws her
into a paroxysm of grief'. He notices the royal children 'always

talking about dear Papa'. He has been led into the rooms of the
Beloved Dead and gazed with astonishment at the Prince's 'open
pocket handkerchief on the sofa'.

A month later Lord Clarendon paid another visit to Osborne,
when he had a long talk with the Princess Royal who had come from
Germany. Vicky always expressed herself without reserve. '—She
said there was no *exclusive influence* (over the Queen). Lady A. Bruce
had more than anyone else, but it was simply because she said "Yes,
Ma'am" to everything and that if she said "No, Ma'am" a few times
the Queen would cease to think her the paragon of cleverness she
now did. I could see there was much jealousy of her (Lady A.) as she
is the only one who has access.' Thus Lady Augusta, carried along on
a current of worthy intentions, drifted into the role of *favourite* and
palace informer, which was her's till her marriage to the Dean of
Windsor three years later.

Clarendon during this March visit had seen a change in the Queen
who was now anxious to hold the conversation for a long time.
Prince Albert's name constantly recurred. '—Acts as if he was in the
next room, indeed it was difficult not to think that he was so, for
everything was set out on his table, the blotting book open, pen
upon it, his watch going.' The Princess Royal had told him many
details, which, he assured his correspondent, were *too long for a letter*,
about 'the extreme difficulty there was in managing her (the Queen),
or in the slightest degree contradicting her'.

Yet at this very time there had appeared at Osborne, almost
unnoticed, a person who was beginning to manage the Queen by a
method all his own. John Brown arrived at Osborne early in March.
Nobody knows who thought of summoning him, or if that person
seriously believed that his coming might cause a change for the better
in the Queen. One bright, frosty morning when the sweeping lawns
of Osborne glistened whitely, the Queen had looked down from a
window. She saw John Brown in his kilt striding through the
grounds leading 'dear little Loch-na-gar', her Highland pony,
harnessed into her own tiny pony carriage in which she used to drive
herself at Balmoral. The shock must have made her heart turn over,

taking her back to the old, glorious happy days in the Highlands. Had not Albert himself chosen John Brown to be her personal outdoor servant? It was said that the smile which lit the Queen's face was the first which had been seen since that dreadful night.

She had hurried on her outdoor things and gone down to greet Brown. Then he had helped her into the little trap. Excitement had made her animated and active. But suddenly she slumped into the cushions like a pale invalid, listlessly fingering the reins and the whip for old times' sake. Brown was to lead her. She could not bear to drive. Yet she was still smiling. She turned to Lady Augusta, who had followed her out, and said it was unnecessary for her to accompany them. Up to that time the Queen had scarcely left the Osborne terraces. They crawled slowly away with the Queen sitting very still among her cushions and with John Brown turning his head occasionally to speak to her. They disappeared among the trees, and a considerable time had elapsed before word was brought to the Ladies drawing-room that the Queen had returned to the house.

John Brown was thirty-five, with red-gold hair and beard and a precisely shaven upper lip, handsome in a big, scrubbed, leathery sort of Highland way. His eyes were remarkable, fierce and kindly, gentle and flaming: but who among the aristocratic Household noticed the eyes of a kilted crofter, faintly odiferous no doubt of stale sweat, who lived among the grooms? But within a month of his coming things wore a different aspect. People were watching the strange man brought down from the Highlands to 'please' the Queen.

When the Queen, outward bound, stepped over her threshold there were often Ladies fluttering about her, anxious to establish their right to attend her, since Lady Augusta seemed too often to cheat them of that honour upstairs. Gentlemen appeared, too, bearing cushions, shawls, mantles, rugs. The Gentlemen expected the Ladies to take the articles from them and settle the Queen in her seat. Brown, without a word, snatched everything from the Gentlemen and shouldering the Ladies aside himself attended to the Queen.

All the articles were briskly set in place. His thick brown hands

poked, prodded and shifted the royal person. Without invitation the
man actually talked familiarly to the Queen as he worked. He had
been seen to adjust the buttons on the Queen's fur jacket and
straighten the collar, his mistress regarding him with an amiable
smile. One morning he told her that her hat was crooked, and she
adjusted it because it looked as if he meant to do this for her.

At times the things Brown growled at the Queen sounded like an
order:

'—Take me arm, 'tis slippery,' was no way to address the
Sovereign.

People who carried instructions to 'Mr Brown' from the Queen –
why did she call him 'Mr Brown'? – complained of his rudeness and
his off-hand manner. There was no respect in the man for anybody.
He never uncovered like the grooms when spoken to; but asked
questions as if he was indignant or doubted one's authority. And, it
was scarcely believable – but could his breath sometimes really
smell of whisky in the morning?

The Queen was not very tidy, rather neglectful indeed, of the
state of her widow's weeds in those early days. Bits of embroidery
silk or cotton speckled the dark cloth, or she spilt things down it.
Brown thought he knew what a Queen ought to look like, and he
took to inspecting her critically and brazenly when she appeared at the
door. When he had her seated his coarse fingers picked specks off her.

Once, the outraged listeners could scarcely believe their ears.
Brown resorted to a local expression heard on his native Deeside.
The Queen was assailed by a loudly indignant whisper:

'What are ye daeing (doing) with that auld dress on ye again? Tis
nigh on green-moulded for want of care, I'm thinkin'!'

With the coming of the Spring weather the Queen took to having
an open tent set up on the lawns. There she sat behind her table with
the State boxes and sent for the Private Secretary. The General,
replacing his working jacket by his frock coat, stepped shivering into
the wind, regretting the greatcoat which etiquette forbade him to
wear. The spectacle of John Brown peering vigilantly from the
recesses within in fulfilment of his function as personal outdoor

servant much irritated him. The man, eyeing his exposed figure with a faintly sardonic smile, seemed to give a knowing ear to State secrets.

But as yet John Brown was only a Court nuisance, regarded as a repulsive, ogreish kind of male lady's maid necessary to the whims of the mourning Queen.

One of the first visitors to Osborne House, other than persons on State business, was Alfred Tennyson, the poet. The strange and deep attachment, lasting till death, which grew between Queen Victoria and her Poet Laureate, and the causes of it, is an interesting side of her story which seems to have gone almost unnoticed.

Although Alfred Tennyson had been appointed Poet Laureate by the Queen at her husband's recommendation ten years before the Prince died, the great bohemian did not in fact ever venture to present himself to his Queen. The Bard lived almost the life of a recluse among his family in the Isle of Wight. He was fifty-three. Daily this massive, shaggy giant in battered wideawake hat and dusty, majestic mantle, haunted the high Downs near the Needles. The piercing eyes, the arrogant nose suggested the eagle to the startled visitor to the Isle as Tennyson like a menacing King Lear flowed by on the sea breeze. He talked to himself, and sometimes growled out the most extraordinary and improper remarks which shocked young ladies. When the spirit moved Tennyson to emerge from his Farringford hermitage for a trip to the mainland, he never missed an opportunity for declaiming his verses in rolling tones to as large an audience as possible.

In February 1861 Tennyson had received a letter bearing the Osborne House address from the Duke of Argyll. This informed him that the mourning Queen was deriving wonderful comfort in her grief by reading and re-reading his poem *In Memoriam*.

It had been the publication of this long memorial poem after the sudden death of his bosom friend Arthur Hallam which had made Prince Albert press the Queen to promote Tennyson to the Laureateship. *In Memoriam* gave Victorians all they could desire. It ranged over land and sea. It was sweet, morbid, rambling, sentimental, heroic and some people thought it deeply religious.

The Argyll letter took Tennyson by surprise. Since his appointment as Laureate he had been honoured by no communication with the Throne.

'—Very touching is what you tell me about the Queen,' came the Bard's answer to the Duke. 'I am of course exceedingly gratified that anything I have written should have power to console one whom we all love: strange that a book (*In Memoriam*) which, when it first appeared was pronounced by more than one clergyman as Pantheistic, if not, as one wiseacre commented, Atheistic, should have such power, but it is very little that words can do. Time! Time!'

The ponderous words of the great poet seem to have pleased the Queen. In the middle of March a letter came saying that she wished to receive him on 12 April.

Tennyson was terrified; but the Laureate must obey royal commands.

'I am a shy beast,' he answered, 'and like to keep to my burrow. Two questions, what sort of salutation to make on entering Her private room? and whether to retreat backward? or sidle out as I may?'

The reply left the Laureate in no doubt that he must never turn his back to the Queen, and at Farringford the frequent spectacle of the huge, ungainly figure walking painfully backwards and bowing indignantly to the empty air stirred some mirth. When he trod furtively across the threshold of Osborne House we must presume that his baggy ratcatcher suit had given place to a frockcoat, since this was the unvarying dress of gentlemen in the Queen's presence.

Tennyson kept no journal; but his wife recorded his experience soon after he returned to Farringford.

'A. (Alfred) was much affected by his interview with the Queen,' she writes. 'He said that she stood pale and statue-like before him, speaking in a quiet, unutterably sad voice. "There was a kind of stately innocence about her." She said many kind things to him, such as "Next to the Bible *In Memoriam* is my comfort." She talked of the Prince (Albert), and said that the Prince was so like the portrait of Arthur Hallam in *In Memoriam*, even to his blue eyes.

'A. said, "We all grieve with Your Majesty", and the Queen replied, "The country has been kind to me, and I am thankful".

'When the Queen had withdrawn Princess Alice came in with Princess Beatrice.'

It had scarcely been a frank interview, but each was deeply impressed with the other, and the Queen at her exit must have seen that she had acted the part of sorrow to perfection before so great a man. By her merciful departure he, at least, had been saved from losing his nerve completely; but he had trembled before her in such a daze of agitation and awe that he scarcely knew what passed. The lively attentions of Alice refreshed him and he lingered for some while enjoying her youthful admiration and the pondering, puzzled, horrified gaze of the infant Beatrice.

Tennyson was far from being uniquely favoured in receiving a photograph of Prince Albert. The Queen was busy dispersing these across the face of Europe. Nor had she lost her own taste for being photographed, more especially as photographic portraits made in this year of Death could appear with an aspect of moving drama. The Queen posed again and again seated in drooping anguish and in carefully chosen attitudes of grief before or beside a bust, a statue, a portrait of Prince Albert, with her eldest daughters and sometimes her sons mourning palely around her.

In July, Princess Alice was married in the Osborne drawing-room to Prince Louis of Hesse, the heir to the reigning Grand Duke. Alice had been engaged before her father's death; but although in the changed circumstances she looked for a wedding shorn of finery and crowded pomp, the grim and lonely exchange of nuptial vows arranged for her in the Osborne drawing-room by her mother was rather less than this deserving Princess had expected, or her late Papa would have desired. Nor can the subdued tone of the wedding luncheon partaken of by the newly-weds in the sole company of the Queen have been anything but painful to the Hessian bridegroom. But this bearded young giant had a sense of humour and was able to take a strong liking for his strange mother-in-law and to earn her lasting affection.

By the unavoidable marriage of Alice the Queen recognized that she had lost the services of an extremely useful daughter. She did not want this to happen again. Her liking for her new son-in-law, who naturally had to return to Germany, had put a clever notion into her head. A *married* daughter with a resident husband – a handsome and amiable young man with no ties who would devote his days to his mother-in-law – would be quite ideal.

'—A married daughter I *must* have living with me, and must *not* be left constantly to look about for help . . . which is too dreadful! I intend to look out in a year or two for a young, sensible Prince for Lenchen (Helena) to marry, who can during *my lifetime* make my house his *principal* home. Lenchen is so useful—'

This ambition of the Queen's, destined to be thwarted by one independent-minded daughter after another, would only be achieved when Baby Beatrice had almost reached her thirties.

The Queen was either convinced, or pretended to be convinced, that she would soon join her husband in heaven, and this obsession naturally made her feel that human affairs in general, and the affairs of the United Kingdom in particular, concerned her much less than might have been hoped after six months of widowhood. As late as 17 April, just before the Household had returned to Windsor, Lady Augusta Bruce, who observed the Queen daily, wrote words to her sister which are illuminating.

'—I am more and more happy about Her mind and soul, though there are dangers and tendencies which point to dangers in the future.'

The Prince of Wales had come home, and the freely expressed fears that his presence would quickly send the Queen into a relapse had proved wrong. By now his mother was putting the finishing touches to a delicate negotiation which would rid her of his near presence as quickly as possible and put him in the hands of a keeper who really might greatly improve him. To arrange the marriage of Bertie to the lovely Princess Alexandra of Denmark, who was said to have such character, was an extremely tricky process; as apart from the fact that the intended bride was a very wilful and obstinate girl, the Danish Royal Family had somehow to be persuaded that the match was an absolutely non-political one with no British obligations whatsoever. This was of vital importance. It was the only State matter in which the Queen deeply interested herself during her first year of widowhood. Terror of what could result from the Danish marriage made her toss sleepless in her bed, praying to the Beloved One as others prayed to God. For no informed person seriously doubted that before long Prussia would try to seize the Schleswig-Holstein states from Denmark – and while she was Queen, Britain must not be dragged into that war. She had suffered enough already.

The engagement was to be officially settled in September by a meeting between the young people in Belgium when the Queen, *en route* for her pilgrimage to Coburg and the birthplace of 'dearest Albert' nearby, would stop for two nights in Brussels as the guest of Uncle Leopold at Laeken Palace. In the meanwhile, the Queen being in good physical shape there was no reason why the family should not go to Balmoral for a short stay. The Queen had a special reason for wanting to weep her heart out in the Highlands.

At eleven o'clock on the morning of 21 August, under a sky of cloudless blue, a silent little party left the grounds of Balmoral. First came the Queen, seated under a dark sunshade in her pony carriage with John Brown at the bridle, then Bertie and the two elder girls on ponies, and Grant and Duncan in the rear. Presently the two younger Princes came panting up to them with moist, guilty faces. It was a solemn hour, for Mama was going to visit the foundations of the great cairn in memory of Papa, which was to overlook the whole valley from the peak of Craig Lowrigan. So wordless and fiercely intense were the climbers that they might have been struggling upwards with the coffin of Prince Albert. Grant and Duncan put their massive shoulders to the back of the frail carriage and Brown caught a shaft and tugged beside the pony. On the summit a few ghillies stood with bared heads and kilts flapping in the breeze. A young nursemaid carried 'sweet baby Beatrice', who had come up earlier. 'The view was so fine, the day so bright, the heather so pink – but no pleasure, no joy! all dead!' runs the Queen's journal.

One by one the Queen and her children placed stones on the

forty-foot-wide foundations, which later were to have their names carved on them, and those present followed their example. They gazed around them and after some whispering began the descent. The Queen walked down much of the rough part of the mountain-side. It was her first resolute attempt at walking any distance.

But the first Balmoral holiday without Prince Albert had less grim moments than this, and John Brown seems to have provided some of them. Perhaps Brown began to feel that he was more than ever in possession of the Queen when he found her under his charge in his native Highlands. When asked by one of his fellow servants about what duty he had on a certain day he answered without hesitation, '*I and the Quane are—*', and the story passed from the servants hall to the Ladies and Gentlemen and eventually through all Britain.

The Queen decided to visit some of her old friends among the cottagers at Crathie, whom she knew would be deeply sympathetic to her in her widowhood. She therefore entered the cottages with a very mournful air. One old Highlander was so sorry for her that he quickly produced cups of neat whisky. It was well known that Her Majesty was a whisky drinker. The Queen refused the whisky. This was too much for Brown, who was in need of refreshment. He gazed indignantly at the Queen.

'Och – wumman,' he burst out, 'ye'd best take it – ye've reason enough with yer sorrows – and hav'ye no got a bit of a cauld!'

The Queen, taken aback for a moment, accepted the whisky with a laugh, and the party proceeded in a shocked but lighter frame of mind to the other cottages.

Brown was given a day off and went to Edinburgh. Doubtless he returned to the Castle well soused with whisky. He had brought with him half a dozen cheap egg cups with a floral design. These he insisted upon presenting to the Queen. She was so touched that she gave orders that she would use one of the egg cups every Sunday morning. One of these incongruously crude objects was still appear-ing with the Queen's Sunday breakfast years after Brown's death.

In the twilight of 3 September a funereal little party, bringing woe with its passage, crept into Laeken Palace. The Queen, with her

daughters shrinking self-consciously behind her, collapsed in floods
of tears in her Uncle's arms. She was always at her most histrionic
with Uncle Leopold, and doubtless the dreadful expectation of the
pilgrimage ahead, and the more immediate bothersome business to
be settled on the morrow were disturbing her. She had travelled as
the 'Countess of Balmoral', but Brussels had not failed to recognize
the black bundled figure pouring with veils at the station, nor passing
through the city.

Bertie had already arrived. His mother's state dismayed him.
Princess Alexandra was to arrive early next morning with her parents
Crown Prince and Princess Christian. Later in the morning there
was to be a meeting – a kind of state interview – between the Queen
and her children and Princess Alexandra and her parents. It was to
take place in Uncle Leopold's writing-room and he would benignly
preside; but the honours of the occasion, the introductions of the
parties, the intimate arrangements were given to Walburga Paget,
the wife of the British Ambassador to Denmark. It was an arduous
assignment for a young inexperienced ambassadress, but it had been
given her because as a close friend of the Christian family she had
been largely responsible for conducting the delicate negotiations
which at last brought the affair to a head, and she it was who had
suggested Princess Alix as a candidate for the hand of the Prince of
Wales in the first place. Walburga was a German, who had been
Lady-in-Waiting to the Princess Royal in Berlin. She had only once
met the Queen, before her widowhood, and was ill-informed as to
the extent to which she had changed.

The first hitch came when the parties assembled in the writing-
room and the Queen sent word that she must have more time to
nerve herself for 'this terribly trying ordeal'. The hour arrived for
the ceremonial luncheon which Uncle Leopold had planned to
cement the morning meeting and the Queen, when informed of this,
declared that she could swallow nothing: the luncheon must go on
without her. She would come down in the afternoon. People ate the
elaborate meal as if they were in a nightmare. Princess Alix appeared
to be almost dying of fright.

That afternoon all assembled again in the writing-room. The Queen had arrived there before them. She was sitting alone in a little closet off the writing-room, and when all were in their places Walburga was to conduct her forward and make the introductions.

At a sign from King Leopold, Walburga opened the closet door. She darted inside and slammed the door behind her. At sight of her the Queen of England had covered her face and burst into uncontrollable sobs. 'Oh, you can understand what I feel!' she moaned. 'You have a husband you love. You can realize what I have lost!'

Walburga had been frozen; but then came pity. She scarcely knew the collapsed woman before her. She abandoned deference, caught hold of the Queen and ordered her to compose herself for the sake of all the others.

The Queen walked into the writing-room. If the company in relief at her appearance failed to perceive the tear stains, they must have sensed that they were in the chill presence of the high priestess of grief. This was one of the first occasions after the death of her husband when the Queen displayed that terrifying majestic dignity which later in her life used to make such an awful impression on all around her.

The conversation, conducted in low breathless tones, since it must never flag, was stiff to the end. But the Queen appeared startled by Princess Alix. She smiled, and was, in fact, enchanted. The beautiful child, so frightened beforehand, was the only one who behaved naturally when the meeting came. It was as if she alone understood the agonizing depth of the Queen's suffering. But Alix's mother the Queen had disliked on sight, possibly because she looked bold and painted her face, and Uncle Leopold was shocked at the Queen's rudeness to her.

Crown Prince Christian, a tall be-whiskered man who was mildly subservient to the rulings of his wife, ventured to require of the Queen a true assurance that her son loved his daughter. This he was given with an impatient and reproachful glare and had no further words with the Queen. It was noted that the Queen seemed above all anxious to explain that Princess Alix would be marrying into a home of Sorrow – she did not say eternal Sorrow, but the inference could be suspected. The Queen retired to her apartments, and the business being satisfactorily concluded, ordered dinner to be brought up to her room. She was seen again early next morning when she departed for Germany and, before the eyes of all clearly demonstrated how pleased she was with Princess Alix. She handed the beautiful child a bunch of white heather which had been picked at Balmoral.

The Coburg pilgrimage passed off rather less bleakly than had been expected by the Queen's companions. The pleasure she derived from her self-inflicted torture seemed to send her home refreshed in spirit and body.

Princess Alix next received a peremptory summons, which angered her parents. She was to spend a month, at least, unaccompanied by a parent and without the Prince of Wales, at Osborne and Windsor. The Queen wished to have some private talks with her future daughter-in-law. Crown Prince Christian could bring over his daughter and return for her when it was time for her to go home.

Fortunately at Osborne and at Windsor the Princess enchanted and enlivened everybody, and her manner of approach to the Queen was thought remarkable in such a young girl. What the Queen said to Alix during those hours spent alone in the royal closet none ever knew. But one thing later appeared evident. The Danish Princess was quite unaffected by the talks. From first to last when she had embarked on her new destiny she did as impulse moved her. She was as charmingly and infuriatingly obstinate as any girl in the United Kingdom – and she never lost the love of her mother-in-law.

That Christmas was bound to be a dreadful time for the family with the first anniversary of Prince Albert's death coming as a prologue to it. But the spirits of the young ones brightened as the black season gave way to the inevitable preparations for Bertie's wedding on 10 March.

The Queen relaxed the mourning for the day of the royal Wedding in St George's Chapel, Windsor. Only the household were to appear in the half-mourning of greys, mauves or lilacs, and the Queen herself would naturally observe no relaxation.

That ceremony, dazzling with colour and pageantry, traditional in its ordering as royal weddings before and after it, was unique, and indeed the most dramatic in our history, by virtue of one weird phenomenon.

Above the Choir in St George's Chapel a strange kind of cage appears in the wall on the left hand side, a forbidding and mysterious bower of dark open-work iron. It has a chilling look today in its emptiness with its aperture gaping blackly but on that day in 1863 the cage with its purple velvet curtains, made to drop or draw back according to the passing emotions of the stricken Queen behind them, may have suggested to some a macabre Punch and Judy show.

Those present in that brilliant crowd gathered to honour the union of a strikingly handsome and happy young couple, recalled in after years not the beauty and movement of the bridal ceremony, but the awful figure of the Queen in the cage, the bright blue streak of the Garter Ribbon slicing irreverently the black weeds, the paper-white mobile face with the unrestrained emotions flitting frighteningly across it, the eyes rolling, the body swaying and the purple curtains dropping and then slowly hauling up to renew the shocking scene.

Alfred Tennyson was not present. Had he been he might well have felt it incumbent upon him to depict the spectacle in heroic verses. The Queen undoubtedly believed that her Poet Laureate was a spectator of the scene. She had given instructions that a ticket was to be sent to Tennyson. This had reached Farringford so late that the Bard, who hated disturbance and hustle, decided to stay at home. The Queen learnt of his absence the same day and was offended. Several weeks passed before she discovered the cause of it, when she was much upset. The Court moved to Osborne, and early in May she wrote asking what she could do for him.

'—Nothing, Madam,' came the answer from Farringford, 'but shake my two boys by the hand. It may keep them loyal in the troublous times to come.'

Tennyson's eldest son Hallam, then eleven, records what his mother wrote of that occasion.

'The Queen is not like her portraits,' she notes, 'her face is full of intelligence and is very mobile and full of sympathy. "A." (Tennyson) was delighted with the breadth and freedom of her mind. We talked of everything in heaven and earth. Shades of pain and sadness often passed over the Queen's face.'

For ten years following that May the Queen's Laureate wandered unsummoned along the wind-swept cliffs of his beloved Isle. His aspect grew more hoary, his garments more unkempt, his speech more unrestrained and his effect on others more overpowering. Then circumstances arose which called to the surface the real sympathy felt for one another by this oddly assorted pair, and the bond grew close and personal.

Meanwhile W. P. Frith, R.A., the celebrated painter of 'Derby Day', was preparing his huge Royal Wedding picture, and had been invited to work in the Reubens Room at Windsor Castle. Frith was most impressed by the good-humoured patience of royalty as sitters, and he has left an interesting glimpse of life in the royal home in the latter months of the second year of widowhood.

Frith reveals that the solemn mourning tone still expected to be followed rigidly at all times in the Sovereign Presence, broke down when the Queen was absent. In fact, the Queen must have been saddened by the *noises off* when her children sought light relief among their guests and the overstrained household. One day as Frith painted in the silent Castle, 'the door of the Reubens Room was thrown open, and a man shouted as if he was proposing a toast at a public dinner, *"The Crown Prince of Prussia and the Royal Family"*. In marched the Crown Prince with his three children, then nurses, and all the English Princesses and then attendants. Fortunately the room is an immense one, or it would have been filled; and of all the rows! – those children shouting, laughing, and romping with the Princesses . . .'

Before Christmas that year the Queen lost the services of Lady Augusta Bruce when she married Dean Stanley of Windsor: a person whom up to that time was much approved of by the Queen. This autumn had been uncomfortable for Lady Augusta, because she could not make up her somewhat virginal mind about a late marriage, and because the dread necessity of informing the Queen of her desire to marry hung over her like a thundercloud. Lady Augusta was perhaps the only true woman friend the Queen ever had; yet even with her there appears to have been a calculating element in the Queen's attachment.

Her words when she finally discovered the truth disclosed no soft feelings concerning her friend's future happiness:

'—My dear Lady Augusta, at forty-one, without a previous long engagement, has, most unnecessarily, decided to marry. It has been my *greatest sorrow* and trial since my Misfortune! I thought she never would leave me!'

To Lady Augusta herself she said:

'He (Dean Stanley) is a very unselfish man. I shall stipulate that you are to be a great deal with me afterwards!'

'That,' remarked the kind-hearted Lady Augusta to her sister, was 'a very dear notion, and sweet, not perhaps practicable.'

When Lady Augusta settled into the Windsor Deanery there was nobody on the female side at Court whom the Queen really liked, except in so far as they would amiably drudge for her morning, noon and night. The Queen as a result became a bully and a merciless tyrant, and her Gentlemen, although they might be cynical and even hilarious about her in their own rooms, were as terrified and disturbed as the Ladies.

One of the strangest aspects of Queen Victoria is the manner in which after Prince Albert's death she began to develop a volcanic force of personality, that in the middle sixties was so electric scarcely a living being could approach her – indeed, come within sight of her – without feeling a shock of impact which continued to tingle while in the Presence.

When, early in 1865, the Queen promoted John Brown to be her *indoor servant at all times* she had a new manager, who seemed free to use or abuse his power as whim took him. If Brown was up to that time a Court joke in bad taste, he was definitely set on his road to becoming the national bogeyman, the sinister Rasputin behind the mid-Victorian Throne.

5

Shades in a Black and Brown Court II: 'Eliza is Roaring Well!'

I N the summer of 1866 Princess Helena married Prince Christian
of Schleswig-Holstein. The wedding was a family ceremony in
Whippenham parish Church, Isle of Wight, and the prevailing
tone was considerably warmer than at Alice's marriage in the
Osborne drawing-room. The Queen was in a sunny mood; for
she had discovered Christian for 'Lenchen'– she had arranged it all.
The fact that 'dear Lenchen' was obviously overjoyed with her most
eminently suitable bridegroom made everything additionally
delightful.

Thanks to the Prussians – generally speaking 'an odious people' –
the Queen surmised that she had found the perfect son-in-law in
Christian. He was a Stateless Prince, robbed of his principalities by
Bismarck who would certainly never give these back; he was almost
penniless, young, handsome, beautifully mannered, most attentive
and apparently without ambitions. The Queen in her beaming
generosity gave the Christians two houses, Frogmore and Cumber-
land Lodge, Windsor Park. It was a mistake: she should have
insisted that they made their home with her at all times, just as she
had always planned.

When the honeymoon was over the Christians joined the Queen
at Balmoral, and it was on the first evening of their stay that it was
revealed to the Queen that her perfect son-in-law had a mind of his
own. The revelation was profoundly shocking and left her
nervously disturbed.

Quite unexpectedly Christian asked her where he could smoke

after the ladies had gone to bed. Nobody before had ever dared mention *smoking* to her. She was well known to be very violent against smokers and claimed to know if any person who wrote her a letter had been smoking at the time. But she did not snub him as everybody expected. She allotted him a little empty room across the kitchen courtyard and ordered a small deal table and one hard chair to be set in it. Nightly when the Queen retired, Christian used to cross the kitchen courtyard to smoke his cigar. Footmen sometimes enjoyed a pipe with him and gradually more kitchen chairs appeared. As time went on this bare room received the title of the Gentlemens' Smoking Room, though the Queen was always said to refer to it with a look of horror as it if was 'an opium den'. Twenty years had to pass before the Queen at the request of another son-in-law, of whom she had great hopes, sanctioned the use of a very remote inside room at Balmoral for the smoking-room and ordered for it some old sofas and arm chairs from the store-room.

At this very time John Brown was known to smoke a pipe in his bedroom, which at Balmoral, after he had become the Queen's inside personal servant, was close to the royal apartments. He may not have shrunk from being seen pipe in mouth about the Castle, for a celebrated press caricature made not long afterwards features his pipe as a prominent feature in the Throne Room. Perhaps the Queen by this time was so besotted with John Brown – news from the royal homes about the *personal Highland servant* was now reaching the public in a tone of highly scandalous innuendo – that she no longer classed him with other men and refused to be aware of his imperfections.

By the middle sixties the weird twilight Court which travelled with the Queen had settled into a routine pattern, and certain men and women who composed it stood out above the others. Since these individuals either continued to serve the Queen for years, or laid down for their successors a manner of conduct adapted to the circumstances of increasing peculiarity with which they had to grapple, attention must now be given to their personalities.

General Charles Grey had been the Secretary of Prince Albert, and since the Prince himself had done all secretarial work for the Queen his work had been of a somewhat mechanical nature, requiring industry and diligence, but little thought and absolutely no guidance or control.

Charles Grey was a stolid-looking man, suggestive of a reasonably amiable bulldog. His nature lacked lightness of touch and also the ironic humour and patience which were so useful to the nephew who succeeded him. The Prince Consort died, and overnight Grey with no little dismay, feeling himself totally unprepared, found himself the first Private Secretary to a grief-stricken Queen whom he believed to be on the brink of insanity. Since the Queen had herself appealed to him, gallantry forbade him to refuse the office.

From that time onwards anything was liable to come the way of General Grey. Apart from the baffling problem which beset him daily of how to manage the Queen, he had to settle all kinds of household matters which filled him with embarrassment. But even he revolted when the Queen one day decided that a young Lady-in-Waiting had been using rouge on her cheeks. The story is told by Grey's nephew, Henry Ponsonby. When the Queen had made up her mind about the young woman's guilt she gave utterance concerning the way of dealing with the offender.

'—That can soon be put to rights,' said she. 'Dear General Grey will tell her about it!'

The Queen thereupon dispatched one of her forceful notes to the Private Secretary's room. The General scanned this illegible scribble with dutiful attention, until its meaning dawned on him. He glared at the paper in horrified silence, then tossed the royal missive into the wastepaper basket.

'—Dear General Grey will do nothing of the kind!' he growled.

At times the General fumed with rage against the Queen. He answered her notes with rude bluntness and when summoned to the Presence to explain his meaning spoke his mind. For that he was respected, but not loved. There were days when Henry Ponsonby found his uncle on the verge of tears.

Henry Ponsonby had been made an Extra Equerry to the Queen at

Prince Albert's death, and during his periods in Waiting he learned much about the duties and the pitfalls in the life of a Royal Private Secretary. He learned also from the tribulations of Uncle Charles how *not* to tackle the extraordinary and unique woman who sat on the Throne if the best results were to be obtained. The General was beginning to grow deaf, which further complicated his life, for it made the Queen excessively angry. The Queen's impatience took the form of seeing General Grey less and less and conducting elaborate conversations with him on bits of paper, which John Brown or the footmen carried to and fro with looks of long-suffering patience. Nevertheless, the Queen appreciated the stolid loyalty of the General and spoke highly of him to others. As for Henry Ponsonby, it was noted that the Queen always seemed pleased when told that it was his turn to come into Waiting. She always treated him in a friendly manner, and perhaps she had already made up her mind about his future.

Another familiar figure in the royal homes, and a prominent colleague of Grey, was tall, bewhiskered Sir Thomas Biddulph, a languid elderly Lifeguardsman known to all as 'Bids'. Whatever happened 'Bids' took it quietly with a gentle smile; but secretly he was often much pained. He had been Master of the Household before Prince Albert died, and since everything ran like oiled machinery he had been very happy in his office. After that things became baffling, burdensome and testing to his peaceable nature. But he irritated his royal Mistress by his unruffled demeanour, and she suggested in 1867 that he should exchange his office for that of the Privy Purse. She would thus see rather less of him and could find a more accommodating Master of her Household.

'Bids' was pleased. His new office gave him an excuse to avoid dreary and prolonged stays at Balmoral and Osborne. The Queen at the same time made a disconcerting discovery. Privy Purse business made 'Bids' efficient and demanding. She had always disliked the Privy Purse. Under 'Bids' she grew frightened of it. It was the one item she could not flout, and she had to obey him. As affairs at Court grew more and more out of tune, and the royal children became deeply disturbed by their mother's behaviour. 'Bids' enjoyed great attention from them, since they believed that he had a braking-power upon her, which neither Grey nor anyone else dared to wield. 'Bids' himself gained confidence, and he allowed himself to become much more outspokenly critical and disapproving of her bewildering and obstinate vagaries.

His successor in the Mastership of the Household, Sir Thomas Cowell, was a soldier of a more zealous and earnest mould. For him the position had worsened. The only sure feature of his post seemed to be that he took the blame for all that went amiss in the royal homes. Brown had started to issue orders whenever it suited him. If challenged he said that he spoke for the Queen. Whatever the truth, the Queen, if appealed to, would be certain to back him up.

The Master of the Household demanded to know why one of his decrees had not been carried out. A footman triumphantly informed him that Her Majesty herself had ordered the exact opposite to be done. If the Queen gave an order or countermanded one she never troubled to tell him by letter or word of mouth. John Brown stopped him in a corridor and brusquely broke the news, or one of the Ladies in passing his room dropped in to deliver a verbal message, which Cowell accepted as correct, but when he acted upon it a letter arrived expressing the Queen's astonishment at what he had done. The royal Governesses, Fraulein Bauer, a plain, sturdy little German, and Mlle. Norele, a Parisian, were both favoured messengers from the royal Closet and both had for prudence's sake to be listened to with care by the gloomy Master of the Household.

After the marriage of Augusta Bruce two resident Women of the Bedchamber, who were young widows of small means determined to keep their posts, wielded the most formidable feminine power for many years in the royal homes. These two, who figure constantly in the royal journals, were Jane Ely, Second Marchioness of Ely, and Jane, Lady Churchill. To the Private Secretary and the Master of the Household – indeed to anyone who wished for the royal approval or the royal assent – these two attractive women were background figures who must never be forgotten.

Jane Ely was of the two the person upon whom the minds of high officials most often dwelt: not because of her capabilities and high qualities, but rather for the lack of these. She was dangerous – not that they were not fond of her. She was charming.

A small, pretty woman with a *piquante* face and a sad, faraway, helpless expression, she lisped and stammered. Jane Ely was terrified of the Queen and adored her. The Queen bullied her mercilessly, and others were used to Jane Ely bewailing her fate and proclaiming that the Queen was 'killing her'. What was she to do? She appealed to everybody, individually and collectively. Invariably she received the same useful advice. Stand up to the Queen! Jane Ely agreed with them and went on as before, treating herself to an occasional bout of peaceful illness when she could bear no more.

Jane Ely always delivered the Queen's instructions or wishes in a 'mysterious whisper', which so vibrated with awe that sometimes it was incoherent. People did not understand, and too polite to cross-examine her did the wrong thing. Storms then raged round the unhappy inmates of the royal Closet. She whispered everything to the Queen, who seemed to weave a hypnotic spell over her, and the fact that the Queen *knew* something usually soon became evident because of her habit of unconsciously quoting the sayings of her intimates.

Jane, Lady Churchill, was quite different. She too was frightened of the Queen, but liked to hide her feelings and if possible avenge herself by disturbing somebody else. To her the Queen liked to entrust the writing of royal reprimands which went down to the offices of the Private Secretary or the Master of the Household. There was no mistaking the meaning in the concise messages of Jane Churchill, which were often ill-appreciated. Some at Court liked her, and all respected her. Even John Brown appeared to feel a certain restraint in her presence.

One notable personage in the royal homes – not strictly a courtier, nor of the privileged circle, yet dearer to the Queen than any man in it – was 'Jenner'. Dr Sir William Jenner, the President of the College of Physicians, who had attended Prince Albert in his last illness without success and after his death had visited the Queen nightly at 11 p.m. for many harrowing weeks. If the accommodating nature of his treatment did little towards leading her back into a state of normality and possibly even encouraged her to linger in a condition of exalted hysteria, the material result for 'Jenner' was that he became an almost constant resident in the Queen's homes for many years.

'Jenner' was a thickset Scotsman with large drooping moustaches suggestive of the army surgeon, and the features of an amiable veteran bruiser. In a bull-like voice he proclaimed his usually violent opinions on everything. He delighted the Queen, and at times diverted her displeasure from the less-favoured. The Household did not feel complete if 'Jenner', wearing his favourite military-style peaked cap, was not striding about full of importance.

Doctors were not considered entirely respectable in those days, and the Queen's order ran that the resident physicians were not to take dinner with the Household, but to be served in their own rooms. This did not suit the Queen's favourite physician. Without invitation he soon became the life and soul of the Household dinners with his wild politics and colourful notions, his gusto for argumentation and sharp differences of opinion. When the doctor was present the Queen's guests, especially foreign royalty, were bewildered by thundering verbal broadsides of the most indiscreet kind, which unaccountably set the Queen laughing.

Sir William Jenner came to be thought of as the Queen's medical ally rather than her medical attendant. This was because after the first few months of widowhood she scarcely ever really needed a physician. Her 'agonizing headaches' which occurred so frequently and conveniently were not taken seriously by the Household as time went on. Henry Ponsonby formed the opinion that 'Jenner' used considerably to affect the Queen by his violent opinions. If the doctor happened to have visited the Queen at a time when some national crisis was taking place, he professed to notice that Her Majesty had suddenly become wild and uncontrollable in her views, as if she had accepted the advice rather than the prescription of 'Jenner'.

In the medical profession an invitation from the Queen's Private

Secretary to do tours of duty as a resident Physician was considered
a great honour. The resident Physicians were expected to attend not
only on the Queen but on the Household and the royal servants. As
a rule the latter duties fell to the honoured visitor, and 'Jenner' took
things easily; for although this doctor was usually one of eminence in
the profession, 'Jenner' saw him in the relationship of a fag to a
school prefect.

One of the physicians invited to Balmoral, Dr Royle, was the
unwitting cause of universal laughter, led by the Queen. This was
one of those evenings when the royal mood encouraged conversation
above a whisper, and it was natural at this sombre table that when
cause for laughter did occur the tense diners became positively
hysterical.

There was a German guest present, Herr von Herff, whose English
was faulty, and that afternoon he had walked over to Glenmuick
with Dr Royle to call on the Mackenzies. Dr Royle had forgotten
his visiting card and had written his name on the back of Von Herff's.

During a lull in the conversation at the royal table the guttural
voice of Von Herff was heard to announce with ponderous
satisfaction:

'This day I left my card at Glenmuick, and Dr Royle was necessi-
tated to write his name on my backside.'

Anything of this kind was likely to be greeted by a musical laugh
from the Queen, which sounded shocking by its unexpectedness to
those not intimately acquainted with her. Humour of a broad or
elementary kind appealed to her. Brown certainly had his value in
this direction, his humour being of the brand called 'pawky' by the
Scots. There was a day at Osborne when the Queen was said to have
been immoderately delighted at one of his uninvited humourisms.
One celebrated Prelate, noted for his High leanings, was possibly too
outspokenly pious and ecclesiastical to please her. When he bowed
himself away with the air of one imparting an unsolicited Blessing
she was ready with her comment.

'I'm sure the dear Bishop when he dies will pass straight through
the Gates of Heaven,' she remarked with a faintly weary sigh to the

Lady-in-Waiting. Brown, a staunch Presbyterian, had been an impatient listener during the interview.

'Aye, mebbe,' he muttered indignantly, and then after a pause. 'Weil, God help him when he meets John Knox!'

From the first visit to the Highlands after the Queen was widowed till the end of her life things did not change at Balmoral, just as the clothes on the Queen's back did not seem to change in all those years. In her first days of widowhood she had appeared in a crinoline gown unsupported by a crinoline, which gave her a peculiar bunched-up appearance, and she was wearing almost precisely the same garment with slightly more decoration in 1900.

People described Balmoral as like a school or barracks. Certainly life at the Castle was as severely disciplined and conducted from morn till night; but in neither of those institutions, as at Balmoral, would half the inmates have lived a hermit-like existence, conducting their daily affairs by means of notes which passed endlessly from room to room.

Years later Campbell-Bannerman, when resident Minister, produced the wittiest and perhaps most apt description of Victorian Balmoral. 'It is the funniest life conceivable: like a convent,' he wrote. 'We meet at meals and when we are finished, each is off to his cell.' Before him, Lord Carlingford had said that a return to Waiting at Balmoral made him feel like an old lag brought back to his prison cell. Lord Salisbury had been downright abusive after his first stay at the Castle. 'I can't disguise my disgust with this place. I'm heartily glad to go!' Lord John Manners after a short acquaintance with the Highland Palace gazed about him with bewildered disapproval and murmured mildly, 'This is a very curious place, and more curious things go on here than I should have dreamt of.'

The Queen was more active when out-of-doors at Balmoral than elsewhere. She drove out daily, always accompanied by John Brown with a bottle of whisky in the rumble, and weather scarcely seemed to have any meaning for her. She rode a great deal and Brown strode along with her, talking in his harsh staccato brogue, but ever watchful of the pony on the rough hill tracks.

From Balmoral the Queen invariably returned to Windsor until Christmastide, and it was in that mysterious quarter of the Castle where the royal Private Apartments lay that most Victorians imagined the heart of their growing Empire. Thousands of visitors to the Castle gazed up at the royal windows in silence. In the sixties many still hinted that a mad Queen sometimes gazed out through those panes. But even if they discounted this macabre tale, here was nevertheless a sinister place with the thrill of melodrama: for when the Queen was in residence was there not always with her a strange Highlander – a man of low birth – called 'the Great Court Favourite' – 'the Shadow Behind the Throne' – 'the Master of the Queen', and in all-male and possibly in all-female companies given another title still more horrifying and unbelievable?

If a visitor looks towards the Castle from the Long Walk he will see the Victoria Tower rising on the extreme right of the battlements. On the first floor of the Tower, and again on the extreme right, is a big oriel window. This was the principal window of the Queen's private sitting-room or Closet.

Although the Closet was a very high room with spacious windows it somehow failed to achieve an air of brightness even when the sunlight was pouring over the multitude of objects which crowded the apartment. A great, cold marble mantelpiece, profusely carved with jumbled mythology rose opposite the oriel window, and below it a cheap brass fender gleamed like an insult. In the fireplace were piled beech logs, the only fuel permitted by the Queen. On the mantelpiece ticked a large Empire clock, flanked by Chinese vases in glass domes, by bronze military statuettes and by a pair of heavy candelabra.

A couch before the fireplace was piled with cushions of many patterns, and in glass cases at each side the objects were massed like an army – animal statuettes, plaster busts, cheap continental souvenirs and old glass. In the middle of the Closet a large table bore a forest of framed photographs, which masked one another; but on inspection not a few were seen to be portraits of John Brown in various poses. Beyond this further photographs crowded the richly

draped top of a large grand piano, with ornaments emerging out of
the display of portraits. An antique, high-backed chair did duty for a
music stool.

Padded plush couches with many small tables, all well-loaded,
lined the walls, and the crimson wallpaper rising to the ceiling bore
a golden floral pattern much broken by an immense array of small
portraits, pictures and photographs. Two crude little bamboo tables
standing near the fireplace were objects of significance. One held a
golden handbell, which the Queen rang when she wished to summon
attendance. The other table was empty, but was placed before her
when she declared her intention of playing Patience.

But the object upon which all gazed upon entering this forbidding
apartment was the broad desk at which the Queen was so often
found sitting. The top of this desk resembled a stall in some fancy
bazaar, so smothered was it with portraits of Prince Albert, of
Brown, of German relations, with statuettes and souvenirs, that the
beholder marvelled at the dexterity with which the Queen picked
from the welter her quill pens in the golden pen tray and her golden
cock's-head penwiper with the scarlet comb, or delved with her quill
at the boat-shaped silver inkwell without splashing the gathering of
portraits. Two bamboo tables flanked the royal desk, holding those
useful articles for which the former had no space: her stationery and
red leather reference volumes stamped with the Royal cipher.

From the Closet a door opened into the Queen's green and gold
dressing-room and beyond a second door gave into the scarlet and
golden bedroom, with its glistening profusion of gilt toilet bottles
and brushes, light chintz-hung canopy bed and picture-hung screens.

Few were privileged to enter the Closet. The Queen summoned
them, ringing her golden handbell which often brought several
people scurrying into the room, and her notes were borne throughout the Castle. But one person seems to have been liable to appear
in the royal sanctuary uninvited at any time. This was, of course,
John Brown. It was said that when he was in liquor he respected the
Queen's privacy so little that he did not trouble to knock, and it may
have been so. Henry Ponsonby was later involved in a scene with the

drunken Brown in the Queen's presence, and she seemed so unmoved by her servant's behaviour that a mere sudden bursting into
her room would seem nothing.

As the sixties moved towards their close the way of life at Windsor
or Osborne seemed scarcely changed since the beginning of the
royal widowhood, except that the Queen now offered a solemn
measure of entertainment to many guests, and her robust health,
unable to find an outlet in the work she might have done had she
been less lazy caused her to expend her spirits in tyrannous behaviour
in the home.

One sign of her vigour was the tremendous appetite she had
developed for one so small. She ate with astonishing speed, which
gave an appearance of greed, and at her dinners she had perfected a
system which guests found disturbing. The Queen naturally was
served first, and on the instant her portion of each course was
finished she laid down knife and fork. As these touched the plate,
Brown, standing behind her, signalled the sergeant footman who
beckoned to his minions. The footmen stepped forward, removed
the half-full plates from the guests and set clean ones before them.
Only one hungry guest bears the honourable record of having
revolted at this arbitary usage. Lord Hartington, naturally an
eccentric, was distinctly annoyed, by the footman's conduct:

'Here – bring that back!' he shouted into an almost church-like
stillness. The footman, turned to stone, gazed in startled horror
towards the sergeant footman. The Queen's voice broke the stillness.
She was smiling.

'His lordship has not finished,' she remarked. 'Put back his plate.'
She then returned to her family conversation at the top of the table.

At Balmoral the Queen permitted the dreary round to be occasionally enlivened by activities of the kind she had much enjoyed in
days when the Beloved One was with her. The full glories – and
ignominies as some thought – of the Ghillies' Balls were not yet:
but when Mary of Cambridge, that Junoesque beauty of the era,
arrived in October 1868 to stay at the Highland Palace in company
with her newly-married husband, the Duke of Teck (they were to be

the parents of Queen Mary), she was not unsurprised by her experience, as she reveals in a letter to her mother.

An open landau met the bridal couple at Ballater, with 'orders to detain us so that we might arrive in the *dark*. This seemed very odd . . .'

When in darkness their carriage neared the black turreted mass of the Castle the mystery was solved.

'A Bengal light at the top of the tower announced our approach, and as we came near we saw all the Highlanders and the Queen's people drawn up in front of the Castle with lighted pine-torches in their hands, which they waved in welcome! The scene was altogether most stirring, and the bag-pipes sounded so well in the open air. The Queen, children and Court were all assembled under the porch and in the entrance-hall to receive us, and Her Majesty was so kind and so affectionate. She took me at once to my apartment (after the Highlanders had given a cheer for us), whence I saw them all dance a reel with their torches, finishing up by dancing round the torches which they had placed in the centre.'

The Tecks' first Balmoral evening was quiet enough: a family dinner of seven, the Queen, Mary and her husband, Helena and Christian, Prince Arthur and someone unspecified. After dinner the men disappeared. 'We ladies sat (*à quatre*) up in what used to be Albert's room, whither the Queen always repairs after dinner. Usually the lady-in-waiting reads aloud, but it being my first evening this was dispensed with. At 10.30 the Queen *congedied* us.'

The next evening was more lively.

'After dinner we adjourned to the ballroom, a fine long room, ornamented with Highland trophies (the royal Stuart plaid hung over swords, dirks, pouches and battle-axes), surmounted by stags' heads framed in oak leaves, the curtains being of royal Stuart tartan. Here were assembled all the household, the few neighbours, and the servants, keepers, ghillies and retainers of Her Majesty, with their wives and families, to assist us at a grand performance of Christy minstrels (fifteen in number), which was most successful. The singing and playing highly creditable.'

Following on this Balmoral occasion the Queen set off on her first continental holiday as the Countess of Balmoral. She had twice been to Germany; but these visits were not 'holidays'. Lucerne, Switzerland was their destination, and there was high excitement before the little party departed.

Henry Ponsonby went with the Queen as Equerry on that trip; and although he is not so amusing and informative concerning this Swiss holiday as he is on the happenings during later incognito continental tours, he does make it plain that their pattern of behaviour conformed more or less to that of ordinary Britons abroad, and that the Queen did nothing to dampen any laughter and enjoyment among her party. Ponsonby refers to this trip as a 'try out' for future royal holidays across the Channel.

John Brown was of the party, and seems to have proved the only morose element. He had already been in Germany where his kilted figure had received a measure of admiring respect in the exalted circles in which they had lived. It was not so, he soon discovered, when the Queen was just a British tripper. Continentals, used only to seeing the pink silk tights of operatic Highlanders in *Lucia di Lammermoore*, thought bare hairy knees disgusting or funny, and in the latter case speculated loudly as to what he wore under his kilt. Brown, shocked and indignant, demanded to appear in attendance in trousers. This the Queen absolutely refused to allow. Probably Brown had a flaming row with the Queen, but he continued kilted and in deep sulks.

During this trip Henry Ponsonby recalls their visit to the great monastery at Engelberg. A service was in progress in the church while the party was being shown round. The Queen hesitated outside the church door, and shot a nervous glance in the direction of her Equerry.

'D'you think it would be all right if I went inside and listened?' she ventured. 'I've never been to a Roman Catholic service.'

Ponsonby saw her point. They knew perfectly well who she was at the Monastery, and, of course, the Swiss newspapers kept an eye on her. His answer made her burst into laughter. He advised her most certainly to go in, even though he supposed there would be people at home who would want to arraign him on a Charge of High Treason for tempting the Defender of the Faith to attend a Popish ceremony. He added that he was not sure that the Queen by such an action would not proclaim herself a traitor and might have to face the consequences. The Queen decided to take the risk and went in and sat down.

Queen Victoria has now been seen during the early years of widowhood both in her homes and in holiday mood. The time has come to examine another aspect of the Queen's personal life in the sixties: the puzzling nature of her relationship with John Brown and the sensational repercussions and speculations and theories thereby aroused. But before doing so, one final glimpse of the Queen in the last year of the decade must be given: because this almost certainly is the most vivid and characteristic impression of her surviving from that time.

Lord Clarendon was favoured by a royal invitation in January 1869, and pithily reports the occasion.

'—We basked for two nights in the Osborne fog of royalty – Eliza is roaring well and can do everything she likes and nothing she doesn't.'

6

The Riddle of Mrs Brown

*T*insley's *Magazine*, October Number, 1868 (edited by Edmund
Yates) – an extract from *English Photographs* (IX), by *An
American* – '*Finally, I am compelled to reprobate the loose manner
in which Englishmen think of and speak about women. They have a bad
habit of telling gross stories over their wine, and often sully a reputation
by an innuendo.*

'*Soon after my arrival in England, at a table where all the company were
gentlemen by rank or position, there were constant references to and jokes
about "Mrs Brown". Confounding her with Arthur Sketchley's heroine in
"Fun", I lost the point of all the witty sayings, and should have remained
in blissful ignorance throughout the dinner had not my host kindly informed
me that "Mrs Brown" was an English synonym for the Queen . . .*

'*I have been told that the Queen was not allowed to hold a review in
Hyde Park, because Lord Derby and the Duke of Cambridge objected to
John Brown's presence; that the Prince of Wales took a special train for
Osborne to remonstrate with his royal mother when the* Tomahawk's *Brown
Study was published; that the Queen was insane, and John Brown was her
keeper; that the Queen was a spiritualist, and John Brown was her medium
– in a word, a hundred stories, each more absurd than the other, and all
vouched for by men of considerable station and authority.*'

Here is a person of the period speaking, a stranger. His words
appear in a good-class family magazine of the day. He is not the only
bewildered stranger who has listened in amazement to the things the
English are saying about their widowed Queen. The Continent is
agog with curiosity. The cyphered dispatches going abroad from the
great London Embassies are stirring dismay among foreign royal

families. The business is clumsy to say the least of it. Queen Victoria is letting down the side.

It is not now ascertainable whether the title 'Mrs Brown' was fixed upon the Queen following the appearance of a mysterious pamphlet entitled 'Mrs John Brown', or if the nickname had settled upon her before its appearance, and the unknown author or authors issued their exposure to satisfy demand among the curious public.

'Mrs John Brown' was privately printed, and seems to have begun at about the same time to circulate very widely in stately homes and servants' halls. If any copies still exist these are probably lying among rubbish in family attics. The pamphlet was said to have been written by someone who obviously possessed some knowledge of certain aspects of palace life. It was, in fact, sufficiently knowledgeable for persons, who spent their lives near the Queen, not to dismiss it as utterly ridiculous when questioned by their acquaintances. They had already expressed themselves pretty freely to their closest friends on the unbelievable things they had seen and heard, and now they were teased and harassed.

The pamphlet declared that the Queen had married John Brown at a secret ceremony. If this was so, somebody apart from the principals must have known the truth. The pamphlet did not indicate individuals; but somehow a story was presently going the rounds that the Duchess of Roxburghe was the only woman who had been present at the secret marriage. This tale spread all over the country, and the Duchess henceforward moved in a sinister aura. Frederick Ponsonby (later Lord Sysonby), the son of Henry Ponsonby, relates how many years afterwards when the Queen was dead and the Duchess very aged, one of the younger generation ventured to ask her if she really had been present at such a marriage. She laughed, protesting that she had never before heard the story and that for all those years she had gone about totally unaware of being a notorious person.

It was never discovered who had paid for the printing of 'Mrs John Brown' and organized the distribution of the pamphlet, but a suggestion was made that the money came from the funds of the Republican party, which was active and growing, as might be expected with such a queer state of affairs existing round the Throne. Naturally, while to many 'Mrs John Brown' was a scurrilous joke, there were also many who half-believed or recognized the possibility that its story might be true, and still others who accepted it as a revelation of fact and furthered its legend for many years.

Never from any other source did a hint come concerning a secret royal marriage with John Brown; but, in fact, what was there to prevent the widowed Queen from morganatically marrying Brown if she was drawn towards him by some profound and irresistible attraction, as some thought they had found reason to suspect? Would conscience stop her – the call of royal duty? What depth of conscience had she who year upon year, robust and volcanic, was so neurotically selfish and scornful of her sovereign obligations? *'Eliza is roaring well, and can do anything she likes and nothing she doesn't.'* If for instance in some spiritual way she connected John Brown with the dead Albert, as some suspected, her conscience might have moved her to unite with Brown in wedlock rather than continue in an irregular emotional attachment, upon which she might feel the ghost of the Beloved One would be more likely to frown.

There were those near the Queen who were growing more and more convinced that in her mind Brown had some mystic bond with Prince Albert. It had been observed that when the Queen was troubled and uncertain as to what she should do she would turn with almost pleading eyes towards a bust of the Prince, and then let her gaze wander towards John Brown before uttering a word. Her movement may have been involuntary. She may have been unconscious of it; but there were watchers who experienced a slight chill, an uncanniness in the air, when they saw this and when later on they found themselves waiting for it to happen again. Difficult as it is to believe, there were those who professed to have seen Brown smoking his pipe in the Queen's presence, and we shall find that the cartoonists got wind of this happening. Comic and trivial as it may seem, those who argued that on this account Brown must obviously manipulate the Queen by some extraordinary and supernatural force were not at all unreasonable!

The first Press attack against John Brown seems to have occurred in the form of a mock Court Circular in *Punch* on 7 July 1866.

COURT CIRCULAR

Balmoral, *Tuesday*

'*Mr John Brown* walked on the slopes.

He subsequently partook of a haggis.

In the evening *Mr John Brown* was pleased to listen to a bag-pipe.

Mr John Brown retired early.'

This was nasty, but mild. The burlesque caused much amusement in high circles. *Punch* spoke out from time to time in those days, and it had never been very friendly to the Royal Family from its first publication. It is probable, as was said at the time, that the Queen read this in *Punch* and laughed at it, and it may also be true that the paragraph when pointed out to Brown caused an explosion of rage and bad language. According to the story he blundered into the royal Presence and demanded that the editor of *Punch* should be punished for his insult. When she tried to laugh the matter off he attacked her so outrageously that both of them lost their heads. A flaming row in the presence of others ended either with the Queen dismissing Brown, or Brown roaring out that he would quit the royal service. Something does seem to have happened; for the Scottish newspapers, naturally very interested in the colourful career of Brown, got wind of it.

Some paragraphs in the *Elgin Courant* (August 1866) give a fair idea of what began to be served out to readers of the Scottish newspapers at this time:

'THE GREAT COURT FAVOURITE'

The London correspondent of the *John o' Groats Journal* says: 'I suppose all my readers have heard of the great court favourite John Brown. His dismissal some weeks ago was generally talked about at the time, and I observe that the fact has now found its way into print, coupled with the suggestion of John Brown's probable restoration to power before long. The reason assigned for his dismissal is an inordinate indulgence in whisky, and the restraining of that appetite is mentioned as a likely condition of his readmission. Far be it for me to question Mr Brown's powers of suction. They may rival those of Dicken's character, the elder Weller, and it is easy to suppose that a Highland Ghillie, who has achieved a practical realization of his compatriots' wish for "a Loch Lomond of whisky" will certainly not be a tee-totaller. But Brown's fall has been more commonly ascribed to *Mr Punch* than to any shortcoming of his own. A few weeks ago *Punch* gave the following as "Court Circular, etc., etc.——' "

The ball had begun to roll; but it was not until the following May, when the first number of the *Tomahawk* appeared, that suggestive innuendo turned vicious and the reputation of the Queen reached its lowest ebb. The *Tomahawk* subsequently made itself by its witty and relentless baiting of the Throne and when after a few years people grew tired of buying it to see its latest insult to the Queen the paper went bankrupt. The first issue carried a caricature of Sir Edwin Landseer's painting of the Queen on horseback at Osborne with John Brown at the bridle. The widow's weeds of the Queen were emphasized. Beneath a caption read, '*All is black which is not Brown!*' The drawing was very well done.

Tomahawk's next cartoon, entitled '*Where is Britannia?*' was more daring – and much more dangerous by reason of the emotions it sought to stir up against the Queen. The centre-piece of the picture was an empty throne with royal robes thrown across it. On a table at the right-hand side a tall domed glass cover – a then familiar object as a guard for painted wax flowers or fruit – enclosed the neglected crown on a cushion.

In August *Tomahawk* played on the same theme, but with more sinister effect. A figure had appeared on the scene. By its introduction *Tomahawk's* anonymous artist had perpetrated the most daring and ferocious anti-royalist cartoon ever seen in Britain, or possibly anywhere, in a public journal. Lolling against the vacant throne was a kilted man, coarse-faced, with bonnet set squarely on his brow, his big crossed feet clad in the heavy nailed brogues of the Highland mountaineer. The arm which propped him on the back of the throne held in its hands a clay pipe. The other arm, akimbo on his hip, half hid with its elbow the crown in its glass dome on the table behind. The aspect of the Highlander displayed scorn as he nonchalantly glanced down at the British Lion, which was charging with an indignant roar up the steps at him. The drawing of the High-lander was no grotesque caricature, but a skilful portrait of John Brown with the look of having been limned from life.

If such an insult to the Sovereign appeared today in the Press, questions in Parliament and assurances from the Prime Minister would doubtless be followed by a sensational prosecution. But nothing followed the publication of 'A Brown Study', as this was entitled, except an uproar of bitter laughter. Nobody called attention to it in the House; Ministers of the Crown kept their silence. But they were not indifferent. They were extremely embarrassed and frightened that somebody might publicly protest against it and infinitely worsen the lamentable business by emphasis. The Queen had asked for this. They suspected that 'Tomahawk' with its 'Brown Study' was more or less telling the truth.

Other journals were zealous in supplying the public with much cruder wit and artistry directed against the Throne, and continental visitors gleefully besieged the bookstalls for matter to amaze their friends at home. If it is true that one comic picture depicted Brown seated smoking his clay pipe in the Royal Closet with his great feet resting on the mantelpiece, while the Queen stands regarding him with eyes of happy approval, the cartoon cannot be found.

The Press attacks caused bitter laughter to turn in many cases to deep anger against the Royal Family; and the fact that the Prince of Wales was said to be quarrelling with his mother because of her improper conduct, and practically fighting Brown in the guise of a virtuous St George, only strengthened the public scorn, since he himself was reputed to be neglectful of his beautiful young wife and as loose in his living as the most reckless of bloods around Town.

The mention in *Tinsley's Magazine* concerning the Queen being stopped from holding a Hyde Park review because she insisted on taking John Brown is more or less correct. It was a fact that the Duke of Cambridge and Lord Derby were seriously perturbed when they heard of this and approached the Queen. She had laughed at them, wept with rage, and wildly defied them. Matters stood in a deadlock of dismay and indignation when Emperor Maximilian was murdered in Mexico by his rebel subjects, and the British Court was plunged in mourning: whereby the Hyde Park review could be mercifully cancelled without arousing undue curiosity.

A point has been reached when the nature of this power exercised by a personal footman over his Queen must be examined from various aspects.

There is a noted historian of one of our major universities, who, in the course of a lecture on Queen Victoria, was asked what was the truth about John Brown. In the eyes of the eminent don appeared the look of a slightly disapproving headmaster; but he did not hesitate. 'There was nothing in it!' he announced and turned to the next questioner. The historian had thereby delivered in a nutshell a belief sternly held by many writers on the life of this Queen. While sadly admitting that John Brown did in fact have a real existence as a kind of palace bully-clown, they maintain that there could not 'be anything in it' – for the simple reason that Queen Victoria was Queen Victoria. Yet, the colourful record of her family in their adventures with the opposite sex from their first days on the British Throne onwards, would scarcely seem to warrant an unquestioning assumption of immaculacy in any individual member of the clan. Would, for instance, a foreigner, who if asked, might be expected to give a dispassionate opinion, declare that it was *unthinkable* that a widowed Queen of this family, ill-balanced, hysterical, fantastically selfish and self-confessedly of a passionate nature was incapable by virtue of her queenhood of being emotionally moved by one of her humbler subjects?

There have always been people less puritanically respectful in their royalist opinions, who have declared, 'I suppose Queen Victoria was the mistress of John Brown?'

An answer to that might be – who can imagine the Queen sharing the royal bed with her personal footman, when hanging a foot above his head is a photograph of the corpse of the dead Beloved One, whom she had honoured by an almost Deistic cult? That, at first sight, seems to be an absolute answer. Yet, if the Queen had discovered – or persuaded herself she had discovered – some deep, mysterious link between Brown and Prince Albert, even this macabre photograph could lose its restraining power. There would seem to have been daytime occasions when lovers might have been favoured with privacy in the royal apartments. Few people entered the Queen's Closet except on summons of the golden bell; for they were too afraid of a scolding or of having some extra burden set on their creaking shoulders if they did make an uninvited appearance. Even the royal sons and daughters did not willingly seek their mother's company. We are told that one human being was welcome in the Closet at any time, without putting himself to the trouble of knocking if he was out of the mood for such politenesses. Whatever people thought of John Brown, a time must have come when his goings and returnings on the Queen's service were such familiar sights that they literally happened unnoticed before the eyes of the household.

The Queen throughout the sixties was unbalanced – surrendering herself to hysteria, to moods of morbidity, to volcanic indignations, to strange imaginings, to swift unreasonable impulses – and it may be that a contributory cause following upon the shock of bereavement was her time of life.

Who can doubt after reading the Queen's 'Further Leaves from Our Life in the Highlands' that she loved John Brown as a woman loves a man? Brown is the hero of the book. The Queen cannot stop talking about him. If she had not been besotted with her personal attendant, common sense would have told her that the general public for whom she wrote cared not a straw how Brown had slept on this or

that date, or in what room, or whether his bed at an inn was uncomfortable, or if he was slightly indisposed in the morning(!), or
what he thought of this or the other trivial annoyance.

Brown's conduct to the Queen is another enigma. If his upbring-
ing was humble it had also been strict. His father had at one time
been a village schoolmaster and had written a local guidebook.
Brown should have known how to behave. Why did he act towards
the Queen with such insulting coarseness and boorish brutality,
whilst he tried, at least when he was sober, to meet her needs with
gentle attentiveness? Was this the manner in which he was moved
to declare feelings of love? Rough, forthright characters do sometimes reveal their emotions in this way. Certainly, Brown's rude
manner of service was not that expected nor customary from the
Highland servant, who is – or was – renowned for his natural
dignity, his fine manners and admirable restraint – a man who
though ready to speak his mind plainly to a master on occasion,
always does so in the manner of a gentleman. Brown, whom the
Queen so admired and whom before his death she 'promoted'
officially to the non-existent title of *Esquire*, was emphatically *no
gentleman*, and his ways must sometimes have stirred a shudder in
his fellow Crathieites in royal service.

There are those who try to argue that the attachment between the
Queen and Brown was of a purely platonic nature – such as might
exist between the Mother Superior of a Convent and the regular
visiting priest: a neutral relationship shorn of emotional feeling.

Here is a little story concerning an encounter with the Queen and
Brown, recounted by the late John Barry-Torr, K.C. Though dating
Brown from a somewhat later period, it is included in this place
because it plainly does not suggest the way of persons in a platonic
friendship. On the contrary it infers an affectionate familiarity as
between man and woman.

In 1875 John Barry-Torr was on holiday with his wife near Balmoral. When out on a walk they rounded a bend in the road to see a
few yards off a small empty pony carriage drawn up by the grass
verge. A man and a woman, close together, proved to be the Queen

and John Brown. The Barry-Torrs hesitated in embarrassment, but were unnoticed. Brown was pinning a plaid round the Queen's shoulders. Evidently he must have scratched the Queen's chin with the pin, for she suddenly squealed, and attacked him in no measured language. Brown offered no apology. He gave the Queen a kind of shake, clutched her more tightly and snapped, 'Hoots, then, wumman – can ye no hould yerre heid up!'

This is the only known incident depicting the Queen and Brown when the pair were unaware of being under observation, and it disposes of the possibility that Brown was an exhibitionist, who acted familiarly to the Queen only when others were at hand to marvel at his performance. There can be no doubt that this style of crude address was followed as a regular feature of the odd partnership.

Nor, before dismissing the respectful endeavours of the platonic school of thought, can we forget the Queen's happy contemplation of Brown's periodical exhibitions of drunkenness when Waiting upon her: a fact vouched for even by her Private Secretary. The occasions referred to are those when Brown had no reasonable excuse for his condition, such as he might have at a Ghillies Ball. When in the early seventies the Queen's old passion for Highland dancing revived, and she would accept no man for a partner but the ribald, whiskified Brown, can her bewildered guests of honour; statesmen, aristocrats and foreign princes and princesses, have pondered straightly upon the touching serenity of the royal 'platonic' friendship?

(The author begs leave at this point to break the narrative for a few paragraphs in order to add one personal reminiscence of a decidedly odd nature to the Queen Victoria/John Brown riddle, which readers may or may not think illuminating to what has appeared in the text. The story I have to tell may aptly be called the *Mystery of the Osborne Letter*, and readers will see that they are quite as well qualified as the writer to form judgement on the matter.)

Some twenty-three years ago when I first took an interest in the strange affair of John Brown, whose name was practically unknown except to the elderly, I resorted to a device which often proves very

The Young Queen.
After the watercolour by
A. E. Chalon. While not
the most faithful portrait, this
perhaps gives a better impression
of the virgin Queen as her fascinated
contemporaries thought they saw
her than the better known ones did.
he grace of form, the nimble, fairy-
like quality, the big luminous
es and lively mouth — even a certain
brazenness of expression — are
cleverly suggested in this sketch

The Young Queen rides in
Windsor Park

The Widow of Windsor
After the portrait by A. Graefle, 1863

'A BROWN STUDY'
The sensational cartoon published in *Tomahawk*, 1867

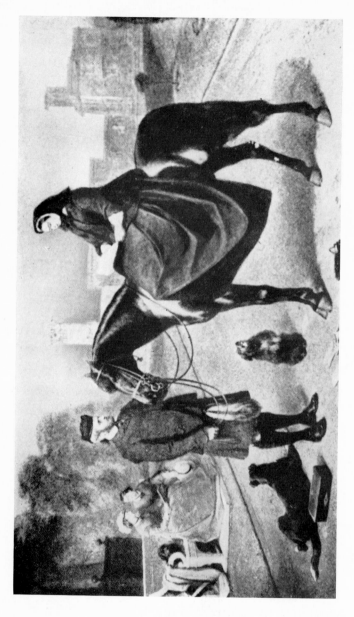

The Queen at Osborne in 1866

John Brown holds the pony. The Princesses Helena and Louise sit in the background. After the picture by Sir Edwin Landseer. This picture was caricatured with the caption, 'All is black which is not Brown!' in the first number of Tomahawk, May 1867

The Queen at her desk at Osborne in the early eighties. An artist's impression

Victoria R.I.

The Queen as most of her subjects knew her in the early eighties.
A popular engraving of the period

The Queen takes tea at Sandringham House, 1889. An artist's impression. The Princess of Wales sits at the tea table. Sir Henry Ponsonby is the bald, bearded man standing behind the Queen

The Queen in the middle eighteen-eighties wearing her miniature crown and veil. This was the headgear which the Duchess of Buccleugh 'accidentally ripped away from her head' at a Drawing Room

'Baby' Beatrice
The only faithful daughter

Artist's impression of a scene in the Balmoral Drawing Room in 1887. The christening of Princess Ena (later Queen of Spain), the eldest daughter of Princess Beatrice and Prince Henry of Battenberg. The Queen holds the baby. Behind her with clasped hands stands the Munshi Hafiz Abdul Karim useful to biographer: an advertisement in the Agony Column of a national newspaper, '*Will persons with personal memories or family records about Q. Victoria's John Brown communicate with—*'.

Some interesting answers resulted; but one large envelope when opened held contents which startled not only the author, but everyone who subsequently saw them. They consisted of a letter typed on a slip of paper, unsigned, no address, only a telephone number, and two photostat plates of a letter with deep black mourning borders. Three items instantly caught the eye at the top of the first photograph: on the right the printed Osborne House address, in the middle the royal monogram of Queen Victoria, and on the left two written words in a running hand, '*Burn this*', with strong underlining.

Another fact at once apparent was that the letter reproduced by the photographs had been torn into small pieces and painstakingly pasted up again on two sheets of old and crumpled brown paper. It was like a jig-saw puzzle, which fitted perfectly and without a fragment missing. Even before a magnifying glass could be found it was obvious that the scribbled words, reproduced rather smaller than as written, appeared to be in the handwriting of Queen Victoria, with the Queen's familiar underlinings.

The accompanying typed letter stated that the sender had a near relation who had held a post of authority on the estate staff at Osborne during the seventies, and that he had received the letter as a curiosity from one of the royal footmen with whom he was well acquainted. This footman frequently carried written messages from the Queen's Closet to John Brown's room. He took these messages to be orders concerning matters in the household, since this was the Queen's way of doing business; but observed that Brown sometimes tore up the messages quickly after reading and dropped the pieces in the wastepaper basket. His curiosity was aroused and one day he obtained the contents of the wastepaper basket, sorted the scraps of paper and finally pasted them on brown paper. The photographed letter was the result of his labours.

The letter, seemingly in the Queen's hand, addressed itself to nobody – nor did it bear a signature at the end. The opening sentences were clearly meant for someone with whom the writer was fairly intimate, some person who made *arrangements*. The gist of these was that '*Helena*' – presumably Princess Helena – and her children would be wanting the bathing machine for the afternoon. It was the office of the person addressed to give the necessary orders. The sentence which followed this matter-of-fact instruction was so incredible, so out-of-context, that one literally gasped, and coming up for breath struggled through it again. —'*Oh, forgive me if I offend, but you are so dear to me, so adored, that I cannot bear to live without you.*' What was coming next? Anything might follow such a moving and abandoned outburst.

Anticlimax followed: with one glowing sentence the writer had apparently discharged the feelings of the heart, and was now concerned with 'the visit to my Scottish capital'. Nothing further of a personal nature succeeded this until the ending – 'your own loving one' and then blank paper down to the black border.

If this letter is genuine, it surely suggests a lovers' quarrel. Only in a case of considerable strain does the writer of a letter jump headlong from the practical to the emotional and as suddenly back again in this unrestrained manner. The Queen and Brown sometimes had violent disagreements – that was well known – and one can imagine Brown after one such occasion and possibly when 'in the whisky' slamming out of the room with the declaration that he had finished with royal service. The Queen, badly frightened but not wholly convinced, decides shortly afterwards to write to Brown one of her routine messages with orders, ignoring the horrible threat; but whatever she intended when she picked up her pen her passion and terror suddenly broke loose in a pathetic plea for pity.

Obviously the photographed letter could be a forgery. A royal footman would be well placed to obtain two blank sheets of the Queen's Osborne notepaper. But what happens next? Whether the footman is a practical joker, or acts with a worse motive, he now has to imitate expertly the Queen's handwriting, and to be familiar with her style and underlinings. Grant that this poorly educated man *might* somehow succeed so far – and without a single spelling mistake

– would he possess a mind of such subtlety that he produced the extraordinary document here described? Surely, his invention would be cruder than this – something more shocking, something to produce a snigger from his fellow servants and cronies in the pub? There are two other possibilities, apart from the letter being genuine. It was written by an accomplice of the footman who was an expert forger, or the footman is a fabrication and it was forged contemporarily or at some later period with some unknown motive. It should be pointed out that the anonymous sender of the photostats could only have expected 18s 6d per plate as copyright fee – at that time – had the photos been reproduced in a publication.

There was at least one thing about this remarkable letter which was certain. It was examined by a number of people, including members of the staff of the author's publishers, and an idea had been put forward that the text of the letter had been made to read as it did by carefully fitting together the torn up scraps of a large number of genuine letters of the Queen. But after scrutiny of the two photographs the unanimous opinion was that, whatever else this document might be, it was unquestionably composed of the pieces of one letter. The fit was absolutely perfect. I rang up the telephone number given on the letter accompanying the photostats and asked for an address to which to return these. The reply was, 'It doesn't matter, they're only photographs. Keep them until they come in useful if you like'. The line went dead.

I kept the two photostats. A war intervened and my family in the meanwhile went to live in Devon. When sorting my papers upon reaching our Devonshire home early in 1946 I came upon the two photostats of the Osborne letter in a buff envelope, and I remember showing these to several people as the oddest experience that has ever come my way as a writer – and I have had several. The photostats returned to their envelope and the envelope went into drawers or cupboards with other papers. Fourteen years later I prepared to leave Devon for London. The bonfires blazed – but the Osborne photostats did not go into the flames. They had gone already. I had no idea where I had stowed them. I only know they had vanished.

The reader has doubtless formed an impression that, apart from any normal feelings of passion entertained by the Queen for Brown, he may well have figured, at least in her imagination, as a powerful link between herself and the Dead. Was John Brown a gifted spiritualistic medium? Was he an unscrupulous imposter, who persuaded her he was passing on messages to her from Prince Albert, and, indeed, presenting her personal – and her State – problems to the other World for a solution? Was Brown neither one nor the other; but, having discovered that the unbalanced Queen for some reason thought him a spiritualistic channel of communication, or even a mysterious reincarnation of her dead husband, was content to make the most of the power and comfort which he enjoyed by the royal delusion? It may even be that the Queen believed that she recognized in the self-opinionated Brown a *passive* Oracle of the Dead, who unconsciously voiced to her the views and advice of the Consort.

Spiritualism was a fashionable occupation in the later sixties and in the seventies, and had the Queen not earlier looked in this direction it would not be surprising if, when there was so much talk about the '*Mediums*' who were claiming to put widows in touch with their late husbands, she should not become hopeful of herself profiting by their occult powers.

One of the stories concerning the circumstances in which John Brown was revealed to the Queen as a medium with the power to link her with Prince Albert is very strange and remarkable. Part of the following details are corroborated – the dating for instance – and if the facts concerning Brown are correct, then an interesting item emerges. *The John Brown scandal was at peak before the Queen discovered that he was a medium.*

On a day in the late sixties a pale youth not yet out of his teens approached the sergeant at the Guardhouse inside Windsor Castle Maingate. He startled the sergeant, who decided that he was soft in the head. He said with diffidence that he had come by invitation to see the Queen. Inquiries proved that he was speaking the truth. His name was R. J. Lees. Later he became one of the most famous professional mediums and mystical writers of the nineteenth and early twentieth centuries. Some of his books, all with a strong vein of religious mysticism, are still honoured by spiritualists, and men of science in his day spoke highly of his powers.

Young Lees had created an eerie sensation in Society drawing-rooms, and it had reached the Queen's ears that in one of the great London houses he had materialized the spirit of the Prince Consort. She had summoned him to Windsor.

The séance which Lees proceeded to conduct in the private apartments so moved the Queen, according to the story, that she invited him to visit her regularly. This, the young man agreed to do; but he was not as yet a truly professional medium, and seeming to be somewhat frightened of his own powers, stipulated that the royal séances should be secretly held, so that the news should not leak out of the Castle to the Press. The Queen herself is believed to have had little concern that her meetings with Lees should be private. She talked about them; and became so deeply impressed after several successful séances had taken place that she offered Lees the permanent post of residential Queen's Medium.

Lees without hesitation told her that it was impossible for him to accept her offer. He explained to the dismayed Queen that his spirit-guide would not allow him to devote his life to the interests of one person. At this the Queen was overwhelmed with despair. The young man gently assured her that her distress was unnecessary. There was a man standing in their presence who, unknown to himself, possessed the psychic power to take his place. The eyes of the medium were upon John Brown. Throughout the seventies Brown, working at first under the influence of young Lees, conducted private séances with the Queen and was her spiritual guide. So runs the tale, and if it is true one wonders if at those secret sessions Brown performed his ghostly office in the same coarse, familiar manner which distinguished his everyday behaviour, and what strange things he uttered to the Queen when in the whisky, and how far his personal prejudices, which were strong both against persons and in politics, can have affected wider issues.

Several years before the last War the author was assured by Miss Eva Lees, the daughter of R. J. Lees, that her father at the outset of his career – that is to say, at the period here indicated – was in close touch with Queen Victoria. During the seventies Lees never saw the Queen; but, said Eva Lees, he again conducted séances for her in the eighties after John Brown had died.

When questioned as to the nature and details of her father's first meetings with the Queen – the writer was already aware of the story of young Lees revealing to the Queen who should be his spiritual successor – Eva Lees politely declined to enlarge on this, saying that she herself was preparing to write her father's life and give all the facts about his mediumistic services to Queen Victoria. This seemed at the time an ambitious task for so elderly a lady to undertake, and it is to be feared that now her manuscript will never reach the printed page.

PART THREE

A Reluctant Queen in the Seventies

7

Hoots in a Stagnant Castle

*E*liza was still 'roaring well' when in 1870 General Charles
Grey, exhausted by his labours, died suddenly, and his
nephew Colonel Henry Ponsonby accepted her invitation to
become the Private Secretary.

Henry Ponsonby had diligently studied the Queen during his
tours of duty as Equerry. He had discovered that while never greatly
exerting himself to please the Queen she seemed to 'answer' to him
more satisfactorily than she appeared to do to many more earnest
persons than he. He had no illusions. He believed the Queen was the
most difficult woman alive, that she would take every fair and
unfair advantage of her position to get her way, and that she would
become infinitely more difficult as the years grew on her.

Perhaps Ponsonby saw the Secretaryship as a challenge; for considering his high abilities he had hitherto wasted his life in the
service. There were devious ways by which the Queen could be
managed, and Ponsonby thought he knew them. In his civilian role
Henry Ponsonby adopted a cool, almost careless manner, which
would have shocked his Uncle Charles. When the new Secretary
presented himself for duty the military mantle had dropped from his
shoulders, and he made his bow in the guise of a bearded, donnish-
looking man, tall, lean, stooping a little, with a look in his eyes
suggesting an easy-going philosopher.

The personality of the Widow of Windsor was around this period
beginning to crystallize. During the sixties she had been utterly
unpredictable; maddening, cruel, hateful, pitiful, impossible. A
process of cooling and coagulation had now set in, and as a result she
was changing from an ogress into a 'character' – a formidable
Sovereign phenomenon like no monarch before or after her. The

very fact that she was so determined not to perform the more popular and spectacular offices of the monarchy, that she saw national demands on her as an impudent menace to her daily comforts, no doubt caused her to assert herself within her royal strongholds in the manner of a tyrannical and pettifogging dictator.

The Queen's determination to 'interfere' in everything had been the growing nightmare of his uncle's last days. Henry Ponsonby surmised rightly that, with a novice in the Secretary's chair, she would become the more inquisitively demanding. He observed with interest that the Queen, while so selfishly unpatriotic in her reluctance to act, was genuinely absorbed in every national problem which called only for exertion of the tongue or the pen.

Every item sent up from the Private Secretary's Office for consideration by the Queen, had to be submitted on a separate sheet, and the papers went upstairs in a locked dispatch box. Presently the locked box reappeared in the Secretary's Office. A paper with the Queen's comments, scribbled perhaps in red or blue pencil, was pinned to each of the original documents. Often the locked box bearing the same papers travelled up and downstairs throughout a whole day, or sometimes for several days. A game of written questions and answers was being conducted between the Queen and her Secretary, with growing exasperation expressed from above stairs and restrained below. All could have been settled in one brief interview.

People accorded the privilege of talking with the Queen, had to be extremely careful if they wished ever to be allowed near her a second time. She was once asked if she would like to hear a lecture by a celebrated Shakespearean scholar. The query sent up from the office returned with the attached comment: '*The Queen dislikes lectures.*' The words typified her attitude to everybody around her – except John Brown. She would not be *lectured*. If she was wrong, if she was ignorant, she did not want to be told about it.

Henry Ponsonby had a technique which he found to prosper with the Queen, and he summed it up wittily.

'When she insists that two and two make five I say I cannot help thinking they make four. She replies there may be some truth in

what I say, but she knows they make five. I drop the discussion.
– But X – goes on with it, bringing proofs, arguments and sayings of
her own. The Queen can't abide it.'

At the time when Henry Ponsonby took over the Secretaryship,
the Queen was in very ill-odour with the general public, and not
only on account of John Brown. 'Bids' – Sir Thomas Biddulph –
aptly summed up to him another reason for national – and Ministerial – indignation.

'The Queen will keep talking as if she is Mrs Jones,' sighed 'Bids'.
'She seems to imagine she can live just where she likes!'

Being a courtier he would not have said 'Mrs Brown', for Brown
had ceased to be a jest to the people of the Court. He was an *un-
mentionable*: men suppressed rising temper in his presence. Frequent
paragraphs in the newspapers harped on the secluded habits of the
Queen, and hinted that this way of royal life could not continue; the
Republican party were taken extremely seriously by the Ministers.
Then the newspapers professed to find a new and grim complaint
against her.

She was 'hoarding' the large sums of money paid annually to her
from the Civil List intended exclusively for ceremonial purposes.
To pay these funds into her own private account, they argued, was
theft of the nation's money. This in fact she was not doing: she
scarcely used any for public purposes, and was paying what she did
use back to the Treasury at the end of the financial year; but nobody
seemed interested in revealing this undramatic truth.

The royal daughters were perturbed about their mother. Wherever they went people asked in a whisper if it was true that the
Queen was about to 'retire', and not a few murmured sympatheti-
cally that they were sure it was the best thing she could do. Vicky
and Alice reported to their sisters that in all the foreign courts
everybody was sure the Queen was preparing to abdicate.

Nothing, of course, was further from the truth.

The public might not be 'fools enough to suppose that the Queen
living up here alone (Balmoral) without Ministers can be governing,' as Henry Ponsonby remarked in a letter to his wife; and Mary

Ponsonby might in her turn tell a friend, 'the Ministers care less and less what they submit to her – I don't blame them' – but the Queen herself honestly thought she was 'governing', and, indeed, martyred and worked to the bone.

Dismay reigned in Ministerial circles in 1871, because the Queen could not be persuaded to come to London for the Prorogation of Parliament. She declared that 'Jenner' had said she was unwell, and that she must leave Osborne for Balmoral several days before the Prorogation date. Members of the Court reported from Osborne that there was absolutely no good reason why the Queen should not attend. Eventually, the Lord Chancellor, a very persuasive man, was sent off to the Isle of Wight. When he left Osborne he thought he had won her over.

But a letter from the Queen soon followed. She had, as she had promised, given consideration to his words:

'—The result of years of experience,' she wrote, 'has taught me that if I yield to mere idle clamour and fancy when NO real important object is at stake, this only leads to further demands.'

According to Henry Ponsonby, John Brown was going about saying that the politicians were making a fool of the Queen and wanted to get her 'up ta Toun' to further their own ends. But all they intended was to save her good name, or at least prevent her from further blackening it. Even Mr Gladstone, usually pretty long-suffering where the Queen was concerned, let himself go on this occasion.

'—A meaner cause for the decay of Thrones cannot be conceived,' he declared to the Private Secretary. 'It is like the worm which bores the bark of a noble oak tree and so breaks the channels of its life.'

This exalted sentiment was fully shared on a baser level by Ponsonby, who did his best to suggest to the Queen that she could, and should, break her journey in London. It was unfortunate for him in his future dealings with the Queen, when in reluctant mood, that he was innocently trying to make her do something which for once she genuinely was unfitted to perform. A painful abcess beneath her arm had to be lanced upon arrival at Balmoral and kept her in bed for days. Thus he was always afterwards at a disadvantage with her and her ally 'Jenner'. The burly Doctor was tackled by Henry Ponsonby, forgetful in his indignation of the danger of attacking a medical man on his own ground, and challenged as to the rightness of his advice to the Queen.

An argument, starting as Ponsonby saw it in sweet reasonableness – 'but surely you could ask her to give London a try for a few days, for the sake of her own reputation if nothing else!' – ended in flame; its salient purpose forgotten in the heat of battle, with the Private Secretary irrelevantly demanding why *She* could '*attend a Ghillies' Ball at Balmoral and not stand a little of a London Ball?*'

The Balmoral Ghillies' Balls were, indeed, an affliction which taxed the patience of more placid courtiers than himself. Quite frequently, during the seventies, Henry Ponsonby would write from Balmoral to his wife at Windsor – she was never wanted in Scotland – complaining of the 'innumerable difficulties' being caused in London because the Queen would not be budged from Dee-side, and the only reason for her lingering that he could see was that Brown had arranged yet another Ghillies' Ball. Political crises and dangerous European crises were numerous throughout this decade, and sometimes the Queen was begged to put forward the date of a Ghillies' Ball by a day or two to expedite her journey South. This could easily have been arranged; but she absolutely refused – possibly because she was afraid of Brown, who was always Master of the Ceremonies.

The only times when the Queen appeared to enjoy herself in company were at the Ghillies' Balls. Whenever Brown decided there should be one the Queen agreed with the eagerness of a young girl, and gaily informed the disgusted household. At these Balls the Queen sat on a low decorated platform with her sons and daughters, if in Scotland, and her honoured guests. The entire household had to attend her and suffer in patience while the noise grew, and sweating whiskified Highland couples in flapping tartans tumbled on top of one another on the dance floor. Since the Queen danced – with John Brown – Ladies of the household and continental princesses could not refuse any bleary and dishevelled highlander who staggered up 'for the honour'.

The *Hoolichan* is a noisy and exaggerated form of Reel. The couples shriek and prance with wild aspect. Brown was always seen swaying at the foot of the royal dais when he had announced this dance. Both the Queen and Brown danced beautifully together – in a Highland competition they might have carried off first prize – but it was not a dignified antic for a middle-aged monarch, and some guests were so upset that they could not refrain from audible comment. When Lord Cairns, the Lord Chancellor, visited Balmoral for the first time he watched in grim astonishment.

'—What a coarse animal that Brown is,' he muttered to Henry Ponsonby, 'I daresay the Ghillies' Ball could not go on without him, but I did not conceive it possible that anybody could behave as roughly as he does to the Queen.'

The Queen, as is well known, was most punctilious about cancelling any kind of festivities when anybody connected with her died. Mourning often gave her an unassailable excuse to absent herself from some distasteful event. But a Ghillies' Ball triumphed over Death on several occasions. One royal decision positively shocked her household. Her son-in-law's father, the Grand Duke of Hesse, died. In one breath she postponed the Ghillies' Ball for three days and imposed full Court mourning for three months.

At Balmoral, especially, the shadow of the Queen loomed over everything. She was the unseen Presence for the most part. Brown was her mouthpiece and impresario: he frequently gave orders without consulting her.

No Lady or Gentleman of the household must leave the Castle in the daytime before the Queen went out – Brown went out when he pleased. This ruling did not affect guests, but did apply to the Minister in attendance. If a Minister sneaked out, and as sometimes happened the Queen sent for him during his absence, he was struck with terror when this dire news reached him at his re-entry to the Castle, so he crept into the Presence with the sheepishness of a boy who had broken bounds.

One little sentence in a letter of Henry Ponsonby to his wife reveals the atmosphere at Balmoral: 'The Queen has gone out for the day with her luncheon in a basket – so I'm off also'.

One afternoon, when the Queen came out to her carriage, John Brown was not waiting for her. It was his daily routine to appear as the carriage reached the door, ascertain that a bottle of whisky was stowed in the boot – the Queen approved of this custom – and wait for her. Then he climbed up beside the coachman and regarded people and landscape with cold hostility. The Queen mounted the carriage with the help of Henry Ponsonby, who had escorted her to the door. She made no remark but consulted her watch. When the Private Secretary could no longer bear this he backed hastily into the hall, turned, and sped upstairs to Brown's room. He was not surprised at what he saw: Brown lay drunk on his bed. He came to his senses, realized what was wanted of him, and tottered to his feet. The picture was not a pleasing one. Ponsonby said nothing. He shut the door, locked it on the outside, and ran down to the waiting carriage. He did not address himself to the Queen, but climbed up beside the coachman and ordered him to drive off. The Queen, as he expected, did not ask for an explanation.

Although the Queen was almost invisible in the Balmoral hive, her orders were felt never-endingly. She daily arranged the menus for the four dinners: the Queen's dinner, the household dinner and that for the upper and lower servants. She even allotted the eighteen riding ponies.

Although none in the royal homes had cause for complaint about their meals, since food was a subject near to the Queen's heart, some odd economies were in force in other directions which were startling to strangers. Arthur Ellis, the private secretary to the Prince of Wales, reveals that in all the W.C.s there were neatly cut newspaper squares threaded on strings hung on nails. His particular table were so resentful of this that they discussed a plan to borrow a packet of cut newspapers from a W.C. and send it in an unstamped envelope as a hint to the Master of the Household, who became more and more bullied and impotent with the years. Another household economy of the Queen's, considered amazing by visiting princes and aristocrats, was that her magnificent footmen, even on ceremonial occasions, had to wear cheap white cotton stockings instead of the regulation silk ones.

The manner of serving afternoon tea provided yet another grievance to royal guests. At all country mansions in that age of country house visits, guests were brought a tea-tray to their rooms. The Queen's guests, after a long wait, were rewarded by the sight of a mildly resentful footman with a lukewarm cup of slopped tea and three lumps of sugar loose on an otherwise empty tray.

There was an afternoon at Balmoral when one of the Maids of Honour met Brown in the hall, carrying a basket. She inquired hopefully if the Queen was having her tea out.

'—Weel, yus and nu!' muttered Brown. 'She dinna mooch like tay. We take oot biscuits and sperruts!'

Fires, or rather their lack, were a sore subject with royal guests in Scotland. Since she could not stand heat herself she thought it nonsense that anybody else should suffer from cold. Early in this decade the Queen had returned half-fainting after a visit to the exiled Emperor Napoleon III and Empress Eugenie at Chislehurst, and commanded Jane Ely to inform their Master of Household that she would never call there again unless they promised to abate their household heating arrangements. When the youthful Duchess of Edinburgh (the Grand Duchess Marie of Russia), came as a bride to Balmoral, she refused to believe a maid who told her that the Queen never allowed fires in the bedrooms. She ordered her fire to be lighted and the windows to be shut. The Russian bride, pining for her hothouse home in St Petersburg, then left the room to warm up. The Queen entered to ask if her new daughter-in-law had all she wished. When she saw the fire she scolded the maid till she nearly fainted, ordered her immediately to remove it in a bucket, and herself threw up the window at the bottom.

Most male guests at Balmoral had an eye to the sporting opportunities of the estate. The horizon, however, was somewhat dimmed for them by the discovery that Brown dominated this side of Castle life, and Grant, the veteran keeper, was merely his minion. Keen fishermen frequently expressed their astonishment that they had caught no fish, although Deeside was celebrated for its fishing. The explanation was that Brown was a keen fisherman. When he awoke in the morning and looked outside he could tell at once if fish were likely to be rising. If so, he decreed for himself a morning's fishing and announced that the river was unavailable to other fishermen that morning.

Brown treated himself similarly to the shooting in the coverts. Royal princes returned with empty bags; then discovered that Brown had cleared them the previous day, and if the Prince of Wales had not been so frightened of Brown he would probably have attacked him when deer-stalking on the hills. Brown's brusquerie and fault-finding reached crescendo in the presence of the Queen's sons, and his sharp eyes flashed with malice.

After a decade of royal service, Brown had certainly become a master in the art of incivility. The Queen's Equerries in those days were usually distinguished Generals, and Brown was suspicious of the breed. General Sir John M'Neil, a stony disciplinarian, regarded Brown much as he would an N.C.O. One morning at Balmoral when Brown came to him with an order for some carriages he was annoyed to find 'the Personal Servant' craning over his desk as he wrote.

'—Go and wait outside. I'll call you when ready,' snapped the General.

'Dinna ye be abrupt with me! – I'm no one of yerre private sodgers,' roared Brown.

A fierce but indecisive scene followed, and Brown departed. On the whole, the General believed he had crushed the man as an officer should crush an insubordinate soldier.

That evening Brown brought M'Neil a letter from the Queen. She offered him a military command in India, which she thought he might like to proceed to forthwith. It was such a small command that the General perceived that he was being militarily demoted.

General Sir Lyndoch Gardiner was a different kind of soldier: the

precise, pedantic, inquiring sort. He had to be 'satisfied' before
ordering horses or carriages. The General infuriated Brown, to
whom he always imagined he was being patient and friendly in
spite of setbacks. When he reached Balmoral to begin a spell of
Waiting, he encountered Brown in the hall; and greeting him with
a warmth he did not feel asked affably after the Queen's health and
her recent doings. Brown regarded him fixedly. Possibly he had
been drinking.

'—The Quane's all right,' he announced. 'Twas only the other
day she says to me, "—there's that domned old ful' General Gardiner
coming in to waiting, and I know he'll be putting his bluidy nose
into everything that dinna concarn him!'

If the Queen had ever heard that she would have rocked with
laughter. She loved to quote the wit of Brown. When Horatio
Stopford, during her Waiting, was ill at Balmoral, Dr Reid, the
physician in residence, suggested innocently to the Queen that a
visit by the Duchess of Roxburghe might 'buck her up'.

'Oh, dear – NO,' laughed the Queen, knowing the two Women
of the Bedchamber hated the sight of one another, '—there would
only be what Mr Brown calls HELL and HOT WATER!'

Brown did not practise abruptness only on people toward whom
he had hard feelings. Henry Ponsonby recalls an occasion at Osborne
when the Mayor of Portsmouth crossed the Solent to call on him
with a request that the Queen graciously attend their local Volunteer
Review. He sent up the Mayor's humble request to the Queen.
Probably the Queen would send down a not over polite note of
refusal; but he would receive this and could soften her words in
transmission to His Worship. He was totally unprepared for what
actually happened.

Engaged in a pleasant conversation with the Mayor, he suddenly
heard the creak of hinges and turned to see Brown's head poking
through the half-open door. Brown eyed the Mayor with a chilling
glance, and addressed himself to the Private Secretary.

'The Quane says – "saretarnly NOT!"' he rasped, and vanished
behind the closing door.

Nothing was left to be said, and Portsmouth's Mayor, looking woefully crushed, was escorted out by the silently sympathetic Private Secretary.

In fairness to Brown let us meet him in a more sympathetic role – indeed in a kind of mock-heroic one – in his routine of attending to the Queen. In the summer of 1875 England was tormented with a mysterious plague of young frogs. In the vicinity of the Garden Cottage, Frogmore, where the Queen was staying, the ground, which at one moment appeared ordinary greensward – was at the next a live, brown, slithering carpet.

Nobody seemed to know where these successive waves of little frogs came from. They came and they went. They were relentless and terrifying in their passing. When the Queen's chair had been set on a tartan rug in the sunlit garden and she had settled with her writing, there was not a frog in sight in the garden. But Brown had been warned, and he waited behind her leaning watchfully on a gardener's besom. He saw the ground begin to move; he saw the gravel of a path turn into frogs; he advanced to the forefront of the royal rug with his besom, and the little frogs, as if the piece of tartan was their special delight, began to close up on it in all directions. Here, there, everywhere, they hopped on to the rug and made for the Queen's skirts. In disgusted horror she watched her kilted champion swirling his besom around him and thrusting off the invaders.

But the frogs were too many for one man; and soon Brown began to roar for aid. Gardeners came running with besoms and took up positions round the Queen, whilst Brown ceased his heroic efforts and assumed the role of commander-in-chief. It was at this moment of drama that the French Ambassador, the Marquis d'Harcourt, making his way gingerly across the bewitched garden, arrived with a low bow before the royal rug; and the Queen, with absolute serenity, returned the courtesy of the distinguished diplomat. A consultation was scheduled to take place, and the Queen, cool and seemingly less disturbed than the bewildered Ambassador, went through with it unhurriedly to the end. This absurd incident stands out as one of the first occasions upon which the Queen publicly displayed something of that Sovereign greatness which later made her the wonder of Europe.

Doubtless, not the least of those intangible pressures, which during this decade were very slowly but surely elevating the Queen to a truer realization of her inborn potentiality for Queenship, was the resumption of her friendship with Alfred Tennyson the Poet. For Tennyson, if his verse has lost its spell, if his unquenchable personal exhibitionism was a smallness, was nevertheless one of the noblest spirits of his time. To him the Queen stood in shining light on a golden pedestal in days when in fact she was still stumbling in fog around the plinth, and his knightly assumption of her Sovereign worthiness, reminders of which came frequently and intimately to her from the seventies onwards, must inevitably have instilled at least an unconscious inspiration towards the ideal.

The Queen had not forgotten her Bard. He had a special place in her heart. Then, in 1873, circumstances arose which called to the surface the real sympathy which existed between them and the bond grew close and personal as the century progressed. In February Tennyson sent a copy of his new edition of 'Idylls of the King', containing an Epilogue addressed to the Queen, to Windsor. In her letter of thanks she declared, 'It would give the Queen much pleasure could she some day, when he is within reach of Windsor, show him the Mausoleum she has raised over the earthly remains of her dear husband, whom he knew how to appreciate, as she feels sure he would admire it and think it worthy of him who wore, "The white flower of a blameless life!" She also hopes that Mr Tennyson will not find Osborne too far for a drive from Freshwater.'

No record exists of the Laureate having stood beside his Queen in the dank and gloomy Mausoleum to which so many visitors were led to pay a grudging homage; but her informal invitation to Osborne inaugurated the first of many private calls when the Queen was in the Isle of Wight. The Queen, who so often was unavailable to members of her own household and to officers of State would always see her Bard.

8

'That Oneness we hear of—' Royal Family without a Circle

PERHAPS it is not so very unusual for a mother who is close to her children in their childhood to be uneasy and bothered in their company when they are grown up. Henry Ponsonby, who was an interested observer of the restrained and fearful relations prevailing between the royal sons and daughters and their mother, was of the opinion that the Queen at heart loved all of them – even the Prince of Wales – 'as much as anyone'. Nevertheless, he would never have envisaged in the seventies a day when the Queen – that 'odd woman' as he called her – had become the most talented Grandmother in Europe; or imagined that desolate band of adult grandchildren who mourned so much more bitterly at her death than did her own children.

The Private Secretary was among those who, on the icy moonlit night of 8 December 1871, waited with the Queen outside the closed front door of Sandringham House, while the bell pealed urgently through the silent mansion, and within the Prince of Wales, stricken with typhoid, struggled for his life. Three nights later the Prince passed safely out of his crisis, with the Queen in a dressing-gown sitting behind a screen and peering through a hole while crouching helplessly beside the tossing patient. It was following upon this anxious event that Henry Ponsonby began to recall happenings since their arrival, and to watch with amused detachment the inmates of the household in this hour of relief.

The house was packed to bursting with royalties and their suites. Until the crisis had gone, all had stood for hours at the foot of the stairs waiting for news. When the doctors declared the crisis past, they retired in all directions to more comfortable occupations. The Queen, happening to descend the stairs, and finding no gloomy congregation at its foot, expressed her opinion of their heartlessness.

On that first morning at Sandringham, when the state of the Prince was very grave, a trivial annoyance had caused the Queen to forget her eldest son's plight. She announced with amazement that all the clocks in the house were half an hour fast, and demanded to know the reason why. The distraught Princess of Wales had explained that because she was always late for appointments Bertie had ordered this in hopes of thereby having her ready at the right time.

'Nonsense, nonsense!' cried the Queen, and ordered the clocks to be set to the right time without further argument. And thus the clocks remained until she left Sandringham; when they reverted to 'Bertie's time', until the Queen's next visit in the eighties.

During her stay the Queen had given all the orders at Sandringham, totally ignoring the fact that her daughter-in-law was mistress of the house. Seasoned inhabitants of the Queen's homes began to feel a very familiar atmosphere of unrest manifesting itself in the Prince of Wales's home. She would have none but Alix in the sickroom, even after the crisis; and the family and their followers, beset by anti-climax and harassed frustration, wandered about wondering why they were still there.

The Duke of Cambridge, with a penetrating brusqueness suitable to the Commander-in-Chief, climbed from cellar to attic, penetrating the bedrooms, smelling in every corner for 'drains' – since drains were the alleged cause of the typhoid – and having attempted to turn out Princess Louise from her 'uninhabitable' sleeping quarters into the corridor, ended by ferociously grilling a startled inspector of the local gas company for his negligence in not maintaining the Sandringham drains.

Henry Ponsonby was involved in an extraordinary scene, which revealed very clearly the odd attitude which the family adopted towards the Queen. He and a companion had passed out of a side door into the garden, when the noise of an approaching crowd reached them. Suddenly, there appeared a clutter of male and female royalty, sweeping down upon them. Their glassy demeanour was that of fugitives with a wild bull thundering at their heels. The Duke of Cambridge led the panting rout, royal sons, royal daughters, royal sons-in-law; and one bleating cry was on their lips as they engulfed the two courtiers and carried them backwards through the door.

'—The Queen! – The Queen!—'

All huddled in a mob, breathless with silent terror behind the door, while the Queen with her Ladies, apparently oblivious of them, sailed into the house. When reporting the hysterical incident to his wife, Ponsonby added in reference to some expression of the Queen's – 'This is that "one-ness" we hear of.'

The Prince of Wales, naturally the most publicized of the royal children and long a problem to his mother, was now in his thirties considered a sad case by many in high places. Some believed that the Queen really would have 'retired' had she truly thought that her eldest son was fitted to take her place.

Teddy, as he was known behind his back, was widely liked. For him the gay life had begun with his marriage; and the most stimulating items in his daily programmes did not include his lonely wife. Probably he was no worse than the average young man of blood of his day – those noble patrons of St Johns Wood and the Haymarket by gaslight – but his elevated position forced him into an underground of murky rumours. In the seventies he presented to the world the general appearance of a bland, pudgy, tolerably haughty, early-middle-aged rip with a tip-tilted hat. The divine right of royal arrogance was growing on him, and his company of polyglot friends knew better than to question the rightness of his plans or opinions.

His naturally hot temper, usually modulated in stress to the pitch of sulks, could be epic and terrifying. The oddest tale of his wrath is so astonishing that it is probably true. He was at dinner at one of those great country mansions which he favoured, when a nervous footman in serving him splashed a spot of creamed spinach on his starched shirtfront. Nobody noticed this accident; but suddenly the Prince was seen to dart to his feet with face aflame. A footman was flinching as if expecting to be struck. The Prince plunged his hands into the tureen of quivering spinach. Then he was sliming this in circles all over his shirtfront and announcing gutturally to a horrible silence, '*I may as well make a complete job of it!*' Kicking back his chair he bolted from the room. Later, in an excellent humour, he rejoined the company.

Distrust of John Brown made the Prince of Wales's dislike for the man more open and vicious than that of his brothers and sisters. Brown, having many opportunities to humiliate him, used them happily.

There was a day at Windsor when the Prince of Wales, never thoughtful, arrived in the royal apartments to see his mother just as she started her early afternoon nap. Brown met him outside the Closet, and was heard to demand:

'What dae ye want?'

'I wish to see the Queen.'

'—Ye're no' seein' yer mither till thrae o'clock. Ye'll need to gang and amuse yersel for an hour.'

The personal attendant pulled a chair before the door and opened a newspaper. The Prince, knowing remonstrance to be futile and dangerous, turned on his heel with a muttered oath.

To Brown is attributed one very shrewd remark about the character of the Prince of Wales. The fact that he neglected his wife and always wanted to be out and about on his own, or to keep his homes full of guests to avoid the boredom of family life, was the subject of discussion among the upper servants. Somebody commented that there must be no privacy at all in the Wales's household.

'Aye,' exclaimed Brown, 'the only preevacy the Prince of Wales wants is the preevacy of the public highway!'

The recovery of the Prince from his desperate illness resulted in drawing the Queen closer to her eldest son; although this was scarcely perceptible on the part of either of them when they were together. But she did begin to suggest to others that Bertie ought to have something important to do.

During 1871 Lord Granville was asked by the Queen to give the

Prince of Wales Foreign Office papers to examine with a view to finding him full-time employment in the Foreign Office. His comments, written at the close of the year – not for the Queen's information – are illuminating as to the Prince's character.

'—He (the P of W) attended the first day (of a Standing Committee). He then came to ask me whether the Committee could not be adjourned for ten days. He had some engagements and so on. I am afraid the Foreign Affairs question would be treated in the same way. If the Queen really desired his opinion he would probably get interested. If he only gets a few bones . . . As to really confidential matters, will they remain secret? He asked me to keep him informed during the (Franco-Prussian) war. One evening I got messages from four different friends telling me to be careful. One of my first notes to him had been handed round a dinner-party.' (26 December 1871.)

In fairness to the Prince, Granville prophesied that if he, in his capacity of Heir Apparent, ever did venture to offer the Queen a suggestion he would be 'snubbed', and he would never do so a second time. This was exactly what did happen. His indiscretion, his naïve inability to hold his tongue, his pathetic urge to boast were misfortunes for which his mother's repressions were partly responsible.

Mr Gladstone, who was much concerned about the Prince of Wales, had one of the oddest suggestions of all to offer under the known circumstances. The Prince of Wales was to be a white shining light at the head of Society – to preside over a kind of 'Arthur's Round Table', to quote the great statesman's own words. Mr Gladstone was certainly right in saying, 'I am convinced that Society has suffered fearfully in moral tone from the absence of a pure Court' – but he could scarcely have chosen a more doubtful leader for it than the Prince of Wales with his Marlborough House set. A time would come when the Archbishop of Canterbury would be called on to initiate public prayers for the heavenly guidance of the Prince and the people around him.

Alfred, Duke of Edinburgh, the naval Prince who was destined to succeed his uncle Ernst in the Dukedom of Saxe-Coburg, was least liked of the royal sons; although he was said to be the most socially accomplished and cultured.

Family 'rows', in the creation of which Alfred with his quick temper was an adept, were well-known phenomena to the Private Secretary, since he was generally buttonholed by one or other indignant member of the family as an intermediary with the Queen. Both sons and daughters shrank from facing their mother when trouble was in the air, and the sons appeared pathetically frightened if they thought they were going to be left alone with her.

Henry Ponsonby gives one example of Alfred of Edinburgh making a fool of himself at Balmoral. Brown uttered some brusque words which enraged him. The Duke roared back in abusive fury. Brown answered as might be expected. There was a glaring *impasse* with clenched fists: the two men turned their backs and strode out by opposite doors.

For a week Balmoral secretly enjoyed the sight of a royal prince and a servant flaunting about and biting their thumbs at one another. The Private Secretary decided that this pantomime had better stop before the Queen heard of it and started a family scene, so he found an occasion to lure the two into the hall as if by chance at the same moment. Standing between them he quickly opened a conversation including them both on some sporting business. They were interested, and then discovered with disgust that they were talking to each other. They parted a little uncertainly but were capable of exchanging a solemn 'Good Morning' next day.

Many said of Alfred of Edinburgh that he had found the wife he deserved. The Junoesque Marie of Edinburgh, the only daughter of Tsar Alexander II of Russia, did not fit into the Court of Queen Victoria. There was something to be said for the bewilderment of this Grand Duchess, used to the glitter and freedom of the Imperial Russian Court; but being spoilt she betrayed her discontent. Marie was bored at all times, and after the Imperial hothouses the freezing misery of British winters nearly killed her. She assured her father the Tsar that the Queen was 'an old fool'.

Arthur, Duke of Connaught, was the Queen's favourite son; but he was no more eager to be closeted with his mother than were his brothers. If trouble was brewing he hid behind the Private Secretary, and always asked his mother for things through him. A rather typical lean, lightly bewhiskered young Army officer of the species guyed on the contemporary stage, Arthur had not much brain; but lesser men considered his company less disturbing than that of the other royal sons.

When Arthur engaged himself to Princess Margaret of Prussia, the daughter of Prince Frederick Charles, the Queen confessed her lack of enthusiasm to her Private Secretary, and her scribbled comments are typical of the notes which poured year in, year out, into the Secretary's office with the outpourings of the Sovereign's mind.

'She (the Queen) cannot deny that she cannot rejoice so much at the event – so few marriages are really happy now. Besides, Arthur is so dear that she dreads any alteration.'

Leopold, Duke of Albany, with his goatee beard, looked like a Frenchman, and this combined with his pale complexion and the cool melancholy in his eyes gave him the most interesting aspect among the royal sons. He was a child of misfortune – the victim of haemophilia. Mildly surprised that he had survived to manhood, living a life of restrained desperation, he endured with harassed but philosophic patience the superintendence which the Queen devoted to every hour of his life. Leopold had to go wherever she went. When he was ill, which was frequently, she would not leave him alone. When he was well she bullied and nagged him and told him what he must do. Only with Leopold did the Queen in actuality display any desire for 'oneness', and it was an uphill tussle stimulating her to further grim devotions.

Prince Leopold, if not the most accomplished of the royal brothers with the ladies, was the most favoured by that sex, and the Queen observing this was filled with suspicion and jealousy. Nevertheless, as from 1875 Leopold somehow contrived to move about a good deal in London and showed some enterprise in making friends. It was he who discovered the incredibly beautiful and lively Mrs Lily Langtry, *the Jersey Lily*, daughter of the Dean of Jersey, and he was unintentionally responsible for her subsequent colourful career as the blazing star of the Marlborough House set, as a sensational leading actress in Britain and U.S.A., without the smallest stage experience, as Queen of the Turf and as legendary friend of his brother the Prince of Wales. Leopold was Lily Langtry's slave, and the story has been told that her portrait hung over his bed and that the Queen was seen standing on a chair removing the picture with her own hands.

To keep Leopold quiet the Queen decided he must have some useful and improving employment, and told Henry Ponsonby to select State papers from the various daily boxes for her son's perusal. Leopold had to make abstracts of these like a schoolboy, although he knew that when the papers reached his mother they went into the wastepaper basket.

After a time the Private Secretary grew cautious as to the selection he made for Leopold. His office time was disturbed by indignant officials desiring to know how this and that had leaked out. Leopold, being lazy or lacking in judgement, often misread the sense of the documents entrusted to him, and then seized some occasion to tell the persons concerned with various political matters what he thought they ought to have done. His 'advice' began to make him most unpopular, even hated.

The melancholy Leopold died early in the next decade, but his last days were coloured with some liberty and happiness. He was married in 1882. The prime mover in this unexpected event was thought to have been his bride, Princess Helen of Waldeck and Pyrmont: a tall, rather plain girl who had taken pity on him. Helen did not care a straw for the Queen, and she, in her turn, decided that the resolute Helen was capable of looking after Leopold.

Of the royal daughters Vicky, the Crown Princess Frederick, was but a passing gale in Britain, closeted for hours with her mother when she did come, her eager voice running on and on, her frankly disturbing beauty distributing vague discomfort around her and somehow suggesting underground politics whatever the subject of her conversation. Alice, until her untimely death in 1878, was only a charming Hessian matron talking of her young family in Hesse-Darmstadt. Helena (Lenchen) had been married four years when the decade opened. Towards Helena the Queen pursued a mildly martyred attitude, having never forgiven her and Christian for their ungrateful avoidance of the *residential* role intended for them.

The marriage of Louise to the Marquis of Lorne, Lifeguardsman heir to the Duke of Argyll, in 1869 had been a sensation. Louise had discovered her husband for herself. No royal princess had married a *subject* since Plantagenet times. Perhaps because everybody expected the Queen to reject the project with scorn, she sponsored it. But Henry Ponsonby says that she rather gave the impression that if Lorne had been an Englishman instead of a Highlander she would have unhesitatingly forbidden it.

It was the duty of Helena and Louise and their husbands to be frequent guests of their mother, but they persisted in regarding themselves as outsiders. Both sisters were engaged in a good deal of public work on their own account, and thereby set a pattern for later royalty. Henry Ponsonby, who knew them well, has expressed the opinion that they were women of considerable personality and attainments who, had they possessed no royal advantages, would have made a name for themselves in any walk of life.

Fair-haired 'Baby' Beatrice entered her teens as the seventies opened. She had been left to the care of carefully selected nannies and governesses in childhood and had little intimacy with her elder brothers and sisters. She was old for her years, and much less *royal* in her outlook than the others, when at the age of twelve she became the subject of her mother's predatory interest. Beatrice was unperturbed by the contact, even happy in it, and was to remain so all her life. If she ever appeared ruffled in the Presence it was at a family gathering when the wind was not blowing fair for her uneasy brothers and sisters. Alone with her mother she was able, while still very young, to cope with things which discomfited the others. Beatrice at the same time developed a sympathetic understanding of her mother and an ability to seem the commiserating ally to all unfortunates who were made wretched by the Queen's wrath or obstinacy.

From the time Beatrice was fifteen, when she was considered old enough to attend Queen's Dinners and mingle in adult company, it became known that the Queen's strongest displeasure would fall upon anyone heard to mention the subjects of marriage, divorce, births or babies in her youngest daughter's hearing. This ban was supposed to hold until the day of Beatrice's marriage when she was approaching her thirties. The veto was not, as was sometimes supposed, intended to preserve the purity of Beatrice's morals. It had a practical motive: her mother did not wish ideas to be put into her head. At last in Beatrice the Queen felt she had found the life-long daughter-companion she had wanted. Beatrice must give no thought to men or marriage. Her mother would look out for a suitable son-in-law.

Yet a rather odd fact arises out of this, which may only be elucidated if Queen Victoria's more personal letters ever emerge from the archives into print.

On 20 May 1874 an extraordinary scene took place at the end of the great Royal Artillery Review before Tsar Alexander II on Woolwich Common. The young exiled Prince Imperial of France, son of Napoleon III and Empress Eugenie, was then a senior cadet at the Royal Military Academy and had been invited as an honour to ride in the Tsar's entourage at the Review. He came in the humble uniform of a gentleman cadet mounted on an uncaparisoned riding-school charger, and looked like an orderly trooper in that glittering train.

The Imperial party led by the Tsar and the Prince of Wales, with the Prince Imperial in their wake, rode from the Review ground. Scarcely had the Tsar and Wales passed in a near silence into the gap in the crowd when a cheer swelled into a frantic roar. Men and women burst through the police cordon and flooded round the Prince Imperial, struggling uproariously to shake his hand. The crowd were acclaiming the young man whom they believed the Queen had accepted as the future husband of Princess Beatrice.

From that time onwards the Prince Imperial was plagued by
hysterical demonstrations and modestly adopted tricks to fool his
usually feminine following. His final departure for the Zulu War –
and a tragic death – was a triumph, such as none other but the
Princess of Wales ever enjoyed, with beflagged railway platforms,
bands and crowds all the way to his port of embarkation. The roman-
tic Victorians assured one another that he was coming back from the
battlefield covered with honour to marry Princess Beatrice.

A powerful widespread belief of this kind could not have spread
abroad and persisted for several years unless the Queen had shown
very marked favours to the French Prince. Yet not only was the
Prince Imperial an ardent Roman Catholic, which in those days
would have aroused sharp opposition against him in high places;
but, more important perhaps from the Queen's point of view, he
made no secret of his set resolve to regain his father's Throne by
stratagem or force at the earliest moment, and in the then political
state of France his dedicated design was seriously considered at high
levels to have a very fair chance of success. The Queen was certainly
deeply attached to the fascinating young Frenchman, son of the dead
Emperor with whom as a young matron she had more or less fallen
in love during a few fascinating days. The Prince Imperial was said
to be one of the only living men who was not afraid of her, and was
actually known at a dinner party to have declared, 'the Queen and I
like one another'.

There is, of course, another possibility. Had the Queen settled upon
the Prince as the ideal resident son-in-law and decided that he must
give up his nonsense about the French Throne and settle down
comfortably to spend his life with herself and Beatrice? The author
has become aware that an absolute conviction still exists among the
descendants of French Imperialist families connected with the
Empress Eugenie at Chislehurst, that such a marriage had been
arranged to take place when the Prince Imperial returned from
Africa. This idea can only have reached them through Empress
Eugenie herself, who was the dear friend of the Queen.

The Queen's journal bears witness to the grief of Beatrice when on a summer morning in 1879 the news of the Prince Imperial's death reached Balmoral. Brown had entered the Closet and bluntly broken the news. The Queen had refused to believe it.

'—Beatrice then came in with the telegram in her hand. I put my hands to my head and cried out: "No, no! It cannot, cannot be! It can't be!" . . . Dear Beatrice, crying very much gave me the telegram.'

No clue is here as to any matrimonial understanding having existed – nothing but bitter grief and the Queen dramatizing it after her usual manner.

Beatrice did not marry for five years after the Prince Imperial's death, when many had decided that she never would take a husband. She found in the end precisely the man to fit her mother's requirements.

PART FOUR

Threshold to Glory

9

At the Villa Clara

As the seventies moved on their way many of those in high places, who found so many good reasons for criticizing the Queen, and who were watching anxiously and more than doubtfully for any signs of improvement – included in their ranks was her Private Secretary – began very slowly to perceive the development of a peculiar and surprising phenomenon. The Queen, far from becoming more and more disliked through her odd goings-on, was actually growing popular with the masses. They came eventually to the conclusion that the Queen, by acting like Biddulph's 'Mrs Jones' or Tinsley's 'Mrs Brown', seemed to the mob to be carrying on rather like their 'old women' might do if they were Queens.

The Queen, in fact, was dramatizing herself in a most original manner and had thereby started herself along the road to royal deification.

But this fact was not apparent to the great ones in 1876 when the Queen quite unexpectedly agreed at last to open Parliament – provided she did not have to wear her crown, which gave her 'a headache', and that her robes were draped around the back of the throne.

For years they had been begging her to meet her Parliament. Now she was coming to do so, they were terrified that such a danger-ous street demonstration was going to greet her appearance that the horse escort might actually be scattered and her carriage overset. A strong body of opinion urged that she must be stopped, or at least smuggled into the House of Lords out of sight of the rebellious populace.

The tone of the tremendous public excitement aroused in London by the news that Her Majesty was to open Parliament was totally misinterpreted by the Government, and the Home Secretary was directed to set Scotland Yard to work to report on the temper of the people in pubs and parlours and ferret out any plots. Their reports that vast crowds were coming out to cheer the Queen were perused with baffled incredulity. But so it was when the great day came: the Queen experienced a triumph. If there were boos for John Brown these were drowned in cheers, and nobody pelted him with stones as had been prophesied.

This was the year when the Queen was cajoled by the fascinating Mr Disraeli into proclaiming herself Empress of India: an action which both raised her own regal morale and furthered her reputation with the crowd. In this year also Alfred Tennyson's historical drama, *Queen Mary*, produced at the Lyceum Theatre by Henry Irving, was the sensational piece. During the run of the play, from the opening night till the end, it was noted not without marvelling on high that nightly one line was greeted with crashing applause not heard at any other point. It was: '*I am an English Queen, not a Roman Emperor—*'.

That May the 'Jersey Lily', under the auspices of the Prince of Wales and Prince Leopold, underwent her presentation to the Queen at the first Drawing Room of the Season at St James's Palace, and her impression of the Queen, then in her fifty-seventh year, is worthy of record.

'—The Queen's wonderful dignity made me unable to realize that she was a *petite* woman . . . she appeared to me to be the very embodiment of majesty. She was dressed, of course, in black with low neck and short sleeves, and her train was of velvet . . . many strings of beautiful pearls round her neck, a small diamond crown, tulle veil, and black feathers forming her headdress. Queen Victoria looked straight in front of her, and, I thought, extended her hand in rather a perfunctory manner . . . not even the flicker of a smile on her face, and she looked grave and tired.'

Prince John of Denmark, the uncle of the Princess of Wales, was a frequent visitor to the Highlands. This amiable, elderly prince had a naïve and innocent air, and owing to his imperfect English twice perpetrated classic howlers at the royal table, which were long remembered with delight.

One night there was a most unheard of occurrence. A lady guest was late and slipped into her place next to Prince John after the meal had begun. She felt compelled to confide the cause of her plight to the Prince. Having locked her bedroom door she could not at first unlock it. The kindly Prince, aware that the Queen was sternly examining the latecomer, was moved to excuse her to the table. A pause in the conversation was filled by his loud announcement, —'So you see, she was *confined* before dinner !'

Prince John was present at a Ghillies' Ball, where he admired the lively performance of the Queen on the floor. At dinner on the following evening he thought it would amuse her if he assured her that she had danced like a spinning top. His vocabulary betrayed him.

'I am agreeable,' he declared with a smile, 'to see that the Queen dances like a pot !'

The Queen when in the mood could be quite jocund herself. She told a story very well and her's were usually about the past. Frequently they were chestnuts well known to the household, but gratefully applauded as light relief. One of her favourites concerned the occasion when she had walked into a crowded State ballroom from the supper-room holding a fork instead of her fan. Another recalled her mother walking along a public street and acknowledging those who recognized her while she held a candle-snuffer in her hand instead of a handkerchief. People listened fascinated to the Queen when she abandoned herself to reminiscence.

One night Alec Yorke, one of her favourite Grooms-in-Waiting, was talking somewhere down the table about Henry VIII's daughter, Queen Mary. The Queen heard vaguely and requested to know what it was all about. He explained.

'Oh,' exclaimed the Queen, '—my bloody ancestor !'

On another occasion at Windsor a prominent cleric was explaining very earnestly to the Queen the nature of his work in the East End slums. He described the plight of wretched families who had to sleep seven to a bed, and evidently expected the Queen to be scandalized at this. The Queen, however, perceived a practical solution which had not occurred to him.

'If I had been one of them,' she declared, 'I should have slept on the floor.'

This was the decade when Mr Gladstone and Mr Disraeli played Cox and Box with one another in the Prime Ministership, and the Queen played hot and cold in accordance with which of the two was in her presence. Mr Gladstone, being a born preacher, was not by nature capable of understanding the Queen's table discipline. One night when he was a Royal guest, everybody but he became aware that the Queen had grown excessively annoyed by his loud and pompous monologue delivered a few feet from her ear. Some were speculating as to what means she would adopt to stop it when John Brown, standing behind her chair, saved her that trouble. He rapped the Prime Minister on the shoulder.

'Ye've said enuf'!' he growled sharply.

Mr Gladstone paused in amazement, and before he could recover himself the Queen launched into an entirely different topic, her face a mask of blankness.

The Queen was pathological about Gladstone. Her viciousness towards him being sometimes childish. In her notes of complaint to the Private Secretary about his enormities the following words and terms appeared: *monstrous – wicked – mischievous – shocking – gone too far – such falsehoods.*

When General Gordon was murdered at Khartoum and Gladstone was considered largely responsible, the Queen sent him a frank telegram. This greatly shocked him, and had he not been *Gladstone* he would doubtless have felt bound to resign. The whole nation knew about this humiliating telegram because it had passed over the wires and reached the Prime Minister in *clear*. Even non-Gladstonians felt sorry for him on this occasion and felt the Queen had overstepped the mark. To quieten the excitement it was given out officially that the Queen's message had gone out in *clear* owing to negligence on the part of a coding official, and this explanation was accepted as fact. Years later after the battle of Omdurman, General Kitchener, the nation's hero, came to dine with the Queen, and she listened raptly to his description of his exploits; then decided to cap his stories with some of her own. The first story she told was about the Gladstone telegram. Gladstone was then in his grave; but she announced triumphantly to the table, as if she hoped he would overhear, that she had deliberately sent the Gordon telegram in *clear* to upset him!

When the Duke of Connaught was about to marry Princess Marguerite of Prussia in March 1879, a list of prominent politicians and their wives who should be asked to the wedding was laid before the Queen. She ticked off the lot except the Gladstones, whom she crossed out. Gladstone was deeply distressed when he heard of this – so much so, that Mrs Gladstone went to his rival Mr Disraeli, then Prime Minister, and begged him to use his influence with the Queen to make her send an invitation. He willingly and confidently agreed to do this. It was the one occasion on which he failed with her.

Disraeli used to tell his friends of the day when the Queen jumped up as he entered the Closet, and he seriously thought as she ran towards him that he was going to receive a royal embrace. After a spell of Gladstone the Queen's eyes shone with tears as her elegant, understanding friend came with a gentle smile to claim his Seals. When the Queen discovered that Disraeli suffered from gout she insisted upon his sitting as they talked; but few knew this at the time because he always replaced his chair against the wall on leaving, thinking his unique privilege was best kept a secret. When he was in Office the Queen weekly posted him flowers from Osborne or Balmoral as a refreshment in his labours, and intimate personal gifts were accepted by the Prime Minister not without misgivings. Undoubtedly, she in her turn fascinated him, both as a woman and as the major problem of his political career; but the breathless flatteries which he offered for her enchantment bred in him a certain fond cynicism to which he sometimes gave expression. 'I never refuse her,' he would say, 'I never contradict – but I sometimes forget!'

In 1877 the Queen startled her household by officially declaring John Brown to be promoted to the rank of *Gentleman*. In future he was to carry the title of *Esquire* on all written communications, and since an *esquire* must rightly hold some landed property she presented him with a large house, *Bhaille-na-Choille*, near Balmoral, for the comfort of his old age. Cynics declared that no man ever did less than he to earn such a title; and shortly after the award of this previously unknown honour, as if to bear them out in their opinion, Brown exhibited his gentlemanly finesse before Herr Koberwein, the noted Austrian artist, who had arrived at Windsor to do some miniature work for the Queen.

Herr Koberwein was met in the corridor of the royal apartments by Brown, who was affable enough. Some room had been appointed as a workroom for the artist and the Queen wished to take him there. When the two men had talked for a few minutes Brown pulled out his watch and scowling at it muttered, 'She verra late the morn—'

At that moment a door opened and the Queen with two Ladies advanced with majestic dignity.

The Austrian bowed low – not so Brown. Standing nonchalantly he shouted out, 'Hey, yourre Majesty, yerre the verra wumman I'm a-wantin' of!'

In the following two years honours came to Henry Ponsonby. He had become a Major-General in the normal course of promotion in 1872, but in 1878 to his office as Secretary the Queen added the Privy Purse, upon the death of his old friend 'Bids'. The new honour was more than his shoulders could bear, and he told the Queen that he must have an assistant. She agreed, and her choice was Major Fleetwood Edwards of the Royal Engineers. Two years later she gave him another assistant, a rather solemn young Artillery captain, Arthur Bigge (later Lord Stamfordham), an officer with no expectations, who owed his appointment and subsequent distinguished career entirely to the fact of having been the best friend in the army of the dead Prince Imperial.

In that untidy office, bare, unimposing and apparently without system, where 'Don't Knock – Walk in' hung outside the door, where work went on at all hours, where nobody ever looked harassed and the most pestilential caller was never turned away rudely, the three soldiers worked together in cheerful, long-suffering harmony. They appeared to enjoy the tremendous task the Queen provided for them.

In 1879 Henry Ponsonby, somewhat reluctantly, was knighted. Evidently by this time he had got into a way of speaking to the Queen pretty plainly, for in the year following his knighthood the Queen called one afternoon upon Mary Ponsonby at their house in the Osborne grounds. A call by the Queen in passing was not unusual; but on this occasior she had a purpose, which she eventually disclosed.

'—You must tell Sir Henry,' she said, 'that when the Queen makes a remark he must not answer, "*It is absurd!*" But please tell him this kindly.'

The Private Secretary was reputed to be almost fearless of the Queen. Yet taken unawares even he could succumb to panic. On a cold spring afternoon when the fire blazed in the grate in the drawing-room at the Ponsonby's Osborne house news came suddenly that the Queen was approaching.

They knew it was not enough to throw up the windows and let in the wind. The fire had to go before the Queen entered the room. Ponsonby dashed for a bucket and was escaping to the lower regions with the flaming embers as the Queen reached the front door.

In the earlier part of the seventies the Queen had not been enthusiastic about continental travel, as she frequently claimed she was in poor health. She visited Baden and Coburg in 1876 and the holiday was voted a dreary one by those who accompanied her. But her stay at the *Villa Clara* in Baveno, 1879, had its moments and left her eager for further ventures abroad. This was the first time she established herself in a static headquarters, and her Private Secretary, as always in future continental holidays, had to accompany her and mingle his office work with that of being an attendant courier as best he could. The events to be described call up an interesting picture of life with the Queen at the *Villa Clara*.

The Queen decided to visit Milan, and Sir H. Paget, the British Ambassador, strongly advised her to give proper warning to the city authorities; for although she called herself the Countess of Balmoral everybody knew her identity – a fact which at this point in her life she refused to admit. All the suite combined to impress on her that the huge crowds of curious Milanese might be very troublesome. She declared this was 'nonsense', and in the meanwhile the news that she had ordered a special train and carriages to be waiting for her in Milan naturally spread like wildfire through the city. When the Queen's special for Milan awaited her at the station and the household – with misgivings – was preparing for departure, the city police remained *officially* ignorant of the Queen's coming, although her bland intention was to circumnavigate the main streets in an open carriage with a kilted Highlander on the box. At the last moment, Ponsonby wrung from her permission to notify the Milan police, but a request for special treatment was forbidden.

It was raining hard when they emerged from the station at Milan. This complicated matters, for the Queen ordered the hood of the carriage to be raised. The crowds, already in the streets and determined for a show, flooded forward, sweeping away odd policemen and fighting to peer under the hood. In a torment of rage Brown sat like a statue with downcast eyes sharing the ebullient honours with the Queen, while outstretched arms pointed at his knees and angry policemen laid about people with Latin fervour.

They alighted at the Cathedral and entered leading a regiment of noisy Italians. When the Queen stopped, friendly Milanese swarmed round her, policemen stumbled against her and Dr Jenner tumbled backwards down a flight of steps. The Queen complained furiously to the Private Secretary at the disgraceful scarcity of police!

At one point in the streets Ponsonby, whose carriage had taken the lead, saw that the people were less thick and wishing to draw the Queen's attention to the pillars of St Lorenzo he alighted and ran back to stop her carriage. It was an ill-judged move. The Queen's face, grim with irritation, appeared from beneath the hood and people deserted the pavement to examine John Brown. Police came racing towards the Queen's carriage and battled to release it from the mob.

It had been almost a wasted day, and the Queen, who was path- etically disappointed, seemed to have no idea that it was her own fault.

On the following day the Queen was to receive an official visit at the *Villa Clara* from the Duchess of Genoa, mother of the Queen of Italy, who was staying at her nearby villa in Stresa.

The Queen considered this a great nuisance. The Duchess had announced her arrival for one o'clock; but the Queen was not willing to forego on this account one minute of her morning drive. She arrived back, very wet, at *Villa Clara* at a quarter to one. All the ladies were wet, and all, including the Queen, went up to change: the Queen declaring that fifteen minutes was ample time for this. Lady Paget, the Ambassadress, was commanded by the Queen to be the first down in readiness to receive the Duchess.

Scarcely had the ladies vanished upstairs when Henry Ponsonby, still in his sporting clothes, was told that a cavalcade had appeared at the foot of the hill leading up to the villa. A scarlet outrider with drawn sword led a stately carriage drawn by four splendid black horses with blue-liveried postillions, escorted on each side by foot- men in long scarlet cloaks. The solemn progress up the steep hill through the pouring rain and mud gave the Private Secretary time to spread the alarm. While the Villa hummed like a disturbed hive and he and Major Edwards rushed to pull on frockcoats over their country trousers, Brown with curses on his lips ran up to the Queen.

Ponsonby and Edwards stood breathless at the front door to welcome the Duchess. The ungenerous nature of the all-male reception puzzled her, as did the Private Secretary's determined efforts to entertain her alone in the drawing-room while her Ladies and gentlemen, having been determinedly separated from her by Edwards, seemed equally bewildered by the emptiness of the smoking-room into which he led them.

Five minutes later the Queen, having outraced her Ladies, walked alone into the drawing-room. The Private Secretary could perceive that *H.M.* was much annoyed; but her Italian was good and her manner gracious. The Duchess was smiling through her perplexity when one by one the Queen's Ladies slipped furtively through the doorway and drew themselves up to make their curtseys. Last came Lady Paget, looking full of distress. After half an hour the Duchess was escorted in state from the villa.

It never seemed to occur to the Queen that the mother of the Queen of Italy would expect a return call of ceremony; but so it was, as was shortly to be discovered by several embarrassed male members of the household from *Villa Clara*. In the afternoon, since the Queen had sent word that she did not require them, Ponsonby, Edwards and Dr Jenner decided to leave their cards at *Villa Stresa* and write their names in the Duchess's visitors book. They took with them one Lady, Ethel Cadogan, a popular Maid of Honour. All were in country clothes and clad in waterproof ulsters as the rain was descending steadily.

In the streets of Stresa a crowd loitered in the rain and advanced with interest as their unimpressive *shay* drove among them. It occurred to none of them that Italians who peered in at the windows were moved by more than rude curiosity at strangers. Chattering among themselves, ignoring the increasing local attention, they neared the imposing royal villa.

Suddenly the appalling truth dawned inside the *shay*. Standing on the terrace before the main entrance of *Villa Stresa* was the Duchess of Genoa, richly mantled against the steady downpour. Her household unmantled and gorgeous, grouped around her. Eight scarlet clad footmen lined the steps with two *valets de maison* in purple. All wore white gloves, and a chamberlain with chain and wand hovered below the steps.

Jenner, pulling down his old cap, muttered, 'Dear me – I'll stay in the carriage'.

Ponsonby, with ulster flapping and cap in hand, splashed past the bowing chamberlain and climbed the steps with an air of confidence.

A fat chamberlain accosted him at the top, and they bowed to one another.

'—Have you the Visitors' Book?' gasped Ponsonby, 'I hope, signor, you are not expecting Her Majesty?'

The chamberlain looked first incredulous, then angry.

'Oh, no, signor,' he answered after a pause, 'we do not expect Her Majesty. The Duchessa only takes a promenade.'

Then he had second thoughts. His black eyes probed the disreputable visitor with a searching glance.

'Does the Queen come?' he demanded, peering suspiciously through the rain at the crowded *shay*.

'—I know nothing, signor,' muttered Ponsonby apologetically, aware that the Duchess of Genoa, who had retired somewhat during the examination, was glaring at him through her lorgnettes.

Having signed the book the humiliated trio scurried humbly away down the steps and slipped into the *shay*, which as soon as the door had slammed crawled off through the rain.

Upon reaching the *Villa Clara* the unhappy party described with indignation the experience they had undergone, and took care that their story should reach the ears of the Queen. But H.M. ignored the hint. She appeared quite uninterested and did not call at the *Villa Stresa*.

10

Foiling a Crowning Indiscretion

EARLY in the eighties an episode is supposed to have taken place in a secluded part of the Osborne grounds which would have been of considerable interest to many of Queen Victoria's subjects, could they have witnessed it, as, indeed, to many of her household.

The Queen – if *The Rambler* of 22 May 1897, a popular cycling journal, is to be believed – could have been seen one afternoon riding up and down on a tricycle and glancing round anxiously to see that no unauthorized person was watching the exhibition. It must have been an oddish spectacle. Rotundity had given to her tiny figure a balloon-like aspect, much emphasized because she persisted in wearing a voluminous black gown fashioned as for the early sixties, but unsupported by the now defunct crinoline. She had, we are assured, a look of exhilaration as she intently pedalled up and down, and expressed herself enthusiastically to the few privileged watchers.

Nevertheless, upon dismounting she declared her decision that it would be wiser if she did not take up tricycling, because, she said, this form of locomotion was not dignified for a Queen of her years. The cause of her making this sporting experiment was, according to *The Rambler*, the sight of a young lady passing her on a tricycle when she was driving on a country road near Osborne. The Queen had stopped her carriage, descended and recalled the tricyclist. After examining the novel vehicle and questioning the rider she invited her to bring it into the Osborne grounds next day and give her a lesson.

Physically, the Queen must have been in good shape at this period for a woman of her years. This seems to be proven by the fact that she took no harm after her prolonged soaking from rain at the great Scottish Volunteer Review on 26 August 1871.

It was raining hard when the Queen in an open landau drove on to the review ground at Edinburgh Castle. This was a tremendous Scottish occasion and the anxious crowds believing she might not appear greeted her with a thunder of applause. All the fashionable carriages which had been closed against the weather were pulled open to emulate the Queen.

Inspection of the lines was cancelled, and the head of the first of the three divisions of Volunteers staggered up through mud reminiscent of the Crimea and hazed in a curtain of rain, which was roaring into a cloudburst. The rain beat like hammers on the umbrellas and the Queen stood clutching hers in both hands with water cascading in a circle around her as the troops went by. First, the Lady-in-Waiting's umbrella buckled and showered her with water: then Brown saw the Queen's umbrella folding. A stream of water splashed her but did not shake her rigidity. He leapt from the rumble and a moment later a lady and gentleman in a neighbouring carriage had their umbrellas ripped from their hands.

The Queen was tossing her crumpled umbrella into the mud as he regained the landau and handed up the umbrellas to herself and her Lady. Again the Queen's started to wilt under the downpour and again Brown set off to find another. This time, to make sure, he snatched several from their surprised owners and, appearing beside the royal landau, threw into it an armful of umbrellas.

When the Queen was staying at Mentone in 1882 a young naval captain, 'Jackie' Fisher – later Admiral of the Fleet Lord Kilverstone and one of the celebrated naval personages of the century – was summoned to dine at the royal châlet on the night before her departure. The reason that the Queen had accorded him this honour was because he commanded her guardship, H.M.S. *Inflexible*, which was anchored in the roads during her stay. 'Jackie' Fisher entered the Queen's home with a fresh mind and his experience is therefore of exceptional interest.

He had been warned that a Queen's Dinner was a very splendid, awe-inspiring affair, and his first surprise was to find the company all crushed together in a 'tiny' dining-room. He noticed that everybody, including Princess Beatrice, invariably said *the Queen*', never '*Her Majesty*', and that all were 'apparently very afraid of her'. Afterwards, in the household sitting-room, he heard from Dr Reid that the Queen's Ladies had been allowed one half-day off during their two months stay, and that nobody had ever ventured from the châlet except when the Queen drove out.

To young Fisher the Queen was very kind, and he was assured that she must have taken a fancy to him. Undistinguished as he then was, she doubtless recognized him as the embryo of one of those 'men of action', whom she so much admired and even deferred to. From the time of this visit he became a member of the band of favoured subjects whom the Queen annually invited for a brief stay.

'Jackie' Fisher's observations concerning the plight of the Queen's Ladies when she was on holiday occurs perhaps as no surprise, but the subject of her general attitude towards them may be carried a little further. No matter what their age, whether widows or wives or spinsters, she considered herself as their guardian.

If at Balmoral or Osborne Ladies of the household, when off-duty, wished to make up a picnic party with gentlemen of the household they were required to ask her permission and to give the names of their escorts.

On the whole the Queen did not much approve of princes or princesses going out for picnics with parties of ordinary persons, unless the latter were in a subordinate or duty capacity, and she once said to one of her teenage granddaughters, Princess Helena Victoria, who wished to join such a party, 'I don't disapprove, my dear, but remember your Grandfather disliked the princesses junketing with members of the household.'

One of the tribulations occasionally endured by one or other of the Ladies was the necessity of travelling in the Queen's sleeping compartment on her train journeys, since she did not like being alone. The Queen was troublesome and fractious at night, and although the dresser, who slept in a communicating compartment, had the duty of rising to look after her, the lady was unable to settle down or close her eyes till eventually the blessed sound of heavy breathing floated across from the royal bed. The only person who seems to have recorded an actual night in the train with the Queen, is her granddaughter, Princess Victoria, daughter of the Crown Princess, who travelled up to Balmoral with her grandmother in the middle eighties. Because of her youth she was a privileged person and allowed to go to bed before the Queen; but in a letter to her mother she describes what was doubtless a typical experience of others:

'. . . I was just dozing off when Grandmama came to bed – and *how* it reminded me of you, my Mother. She looked so clean and dear – all in white – and it took some time before she was settled – the shawls and cushions – then the lamps to put out – then again, it felt too hot – then not warm enough, and in the night – Annie was called many a time – to bring her something to drink etc. – Well, finally we had some sleep.'

It was on Tuesday night, 27 March 1883, that news spread round Windsor Castle that John Brown had died suddenly during an attack of erysipelas. He was fifty-six.

There were those in the suite, both man and woman, who did not hesitate to express their gladness at the report; but not one of them dared go in to tell the Queen. At last Prince Leopold agreed to do so. When he had spoken an awful stillness came over her, and only the tears trickling in rivers down her cheeks betrayed that she was not a wax effigy.

Ponsonby, who could not feel much sympathy with her in the loss of Brown, nor comprehend her grief, says that the shock paralysed both her legs for a time and that for four days she would see no one and put her signature to nothing. Determined that the Queen must not be allowed to lapse into a state resembling the prostration following the Consort's death, he wrote her a firm note practically demanding to see her on State matters at the end of the fourth day. Her written reply, although it agreed to see him, filled him with wonder and proved his suspicions to be not far short of the mark.

'. . . the Queen is utterly crushed,' she informed him, 'and her life has sustained one of those shocks like in 1861, when every link has been shaken and torn at every turn – the shock she has sustained has made her very weak – so that she can't stand.'

Perhaps the passionate hysteria of earlier days was no longer possible with the Queen. The force of her presence soon became manifest once more to all. From the ordering and distribution of busts and statuettes for the royal homes and gardens, and the placing of cairns and inscribed garden seats to his memory, she turned to the preparation for publication of the part of her journal to be called *Further Leaves from Our Life in the Highlands*. It might have been thought that the last person to whom the Queen would feel urged to send her MS. for perusal would have been Brown's worst enemy, the Prince of Wales; but to him it was sent in the nature of a singular favour.

He was no reader, except of newspapers, but a hasty glance was enough to show him that there was too much *Brown* in it. That night he wrote his mother a letter saying that he had been thinking the matter over and he felt *it most unwise for the Queen to expose her private life to the public.*

The Prince of Wales's letter came down from the Closet to the Private Secretary in the Box labelled 'The Queen', a dreaded vehicle of communication used commonly for messages of royal displeasure to resident members of the family or offenders among the suite. The Queen had pinned a covering note to her son's letter:

'. . . strange, considering how much talk and want of reticence there is in his house and how little he keeps anything to himself. It is strange that objection should come from this quarter, where great strictness as to conduct is not generally much cared for.'

An infinitely more serious matter concerning the Queen's urge to authorship was revealed to Henry Ponsonby in a more or less casual note which came down to him in February of the following year. She said that she had written the *Life of John Brown* for publication and that she also intended to publish Brown's personal diary written while he was in the royal service. She added that she had invited Sir Theodore Martin (the historian and author of the three-volume *Life of the Prince Consort*), to write up her MS. of John Brown for her; but he had replied that he could not do so owing to his wife's illness. Then she had given her MS. to a Miss McGregor to edit. This lady had returned the Life, declaring it was ready for publication. The Queen, however, remarked that she was not very happy about the result.

Ponsonby had his chance, and he seized it. He believed it was his duty to get possession of both the Life and Brown's diary as quickly as possible. Accordingly, he assured the Queen that he was quite sure he could find a more suitable person to deal with the two MSS. if she would let him have them and, to his surprise, she at once sent these down to him.

As he sat reading through the documents his blood ran cold. Publication of either of them was utterly out of the question. The Throne had survived the John Brown scandal; he was doubtful if it could survive the Brown publications. He knew he was facing the biggest crisis in his career of royal Secretaryship. Never had the Queen set her heart on a project such as this. He had spent his days in managing the Queen more or less, by a process of blandness and patience, by watering-down and judicious omissions: this time he had got to beat her by fair means or by foul. At least he had a trump card: he had the Queen's manuscripts on his table, and they would soon be under lock and key. He did not know what he was going to do about them: he did know that if the worst came to the worst he was going to defy the Queen and throw the papers into the fire.

The Private Secretary had learnt that frankness spelt royal resentment and opposition disaster. Unsanguine as he was that any sharp remonstrance from him would move the Queen, he took up his pen. This time he felt things were almost beyond him – unless he descended to the ultimate violation; but he would try plain-speaking first.

He started by venturing to bring to the Queen's notice his misgivings of the wisdom of exposing to the British public and to the world, 'Your Majesty's innermost and most sacred feelings . . .

There are passages which will be misunderstood if read by strangers and expressions which will attract remarks of an unfavourable nature . . . and Sir Henry cannot help fearing—'.

It was courteous in its way, and the recipient could not easily pick a quarrel out of it and thereby slam the door against any further approaches; but since no answer came to his remonstrance he found himself in the dark and at a loss for the next move. He received a demand for the return of the manuscripts; but became aware that the Queen wished to avoid seeing him, and discovered also that she was still talking to her Ladies about her projected publications. She might at any moment send down a casual request for her property.

Ponsonby went to Dr Davidson, the Dean of Windsor (later the celebrated Archbishop) who was already vaguely aware of what was in the wind. It was not a matter which in any way was within his responsibility. But the Deanery of Windsor was a royal appointment and traditionally regarded by the family as a very personal one. Probably no younger cleric of the brilliant strata of the Church, who were marked down for higher things, was more admired by the Queen than her Dean, and he might confidently expect her to forward his interest at every opportunity.

According to Dr Bell, who wrote Archbishop Davidson's life, the Dean immediately wrote a very able and tactful letter to the Queen dissuading her from proceeding with any idea of publication. The Queen was bitterly offended and very angry. Had matters rested there, it might well have been that Davidson's cruel disloyalty would have been the spur to make the Queen finally take the bit between her teeth. But the Dean was a man prepared to go beyond verbal protestations.

A message was carried to the Deanery by Jane Ely. The Queen required the Dean to withdraw his letter, since the subject of it was none of his business. Davidson returned a message that he refused to do this – that he objected most strongly to the publication of the books – that if the Queen still persisted in asking him to withdraw his letter he would resign the Deanery of Windsor.

The first that Davidson heard of the Queen after the dispatch of his ultimatum was an invitation to take tea with her which arrived three weeks later. He entered the royal apartments expecting to be the centre of a scene more appalling perhaps than any subject had ever faced before.

But the Queen welcomed him with smiles, behaving shyly like a child who has been naughty and hopes not to be reminded of it. During their long *tête-à-tête*, with subject after subject coming up for discussion, he began to feel increasingly sure of one thing – that the matter of John Brown was not scheduled to leap out suddenly like an ugly Jack-in-a-box. Since etiquette insisted that the Queen initiated and her listener endeavoured to satisfy her conversational advances, the Dean sat wondering to the end and bowed himself out in total darkness. Only afterwards did he learn that the Queen had already given instructions to the Private Secretary to destroy the John Brown manuscripts.

Thus fortunately ended a transaction which prevented the launching of what might have become the greatest popular European literary sensation of the nineteenth century. All the royal families of the time harboured their scandals, more or less condoned by the masses in accordance with their racial outlook; but even the most tolerant of Latins would have gasped in shocked incredulity at a reigning Queen who wrote the life of her personal footman and edited his diaries concerning herself and her Court for public entertainment. As for the Brown diaries, whatever their nature in the form the Queen gave them to the world, one inevitable result must have followed their appearance: everybody would have used their imagination in conjecturing what items the royal editor had expurgated.

In the year of Brown's death, one of the Queen's subjects who had wholeheartedly sympathized with her in her loss was Alfred Tennyson. The Poet Laureate, whom many had reason to think of as a crude, unrestrained old man, knew now how to catch the moods of his Queen. His manner to her was worthy of the whitest knights whom he set at 'King Arthur's Round Table'. He came over to

Osborne to visit her on Tuesday 7 August, and offered consolation
in her sorrow; which was evidently received with deep gratitude.
But this fact is less apparent in the description of his visit in the
Queen's journal than in his Tennysonian letter to her upon his
return to Farringford:

'After luncheon saw the great Poet Tennyson in dearest Albert's
room for nearly an hour,' notes the Queen, 'and most interesting it
was. He is grown very old, his eyesight much impaired. But he was
very kind. Asked him to sit down . . . I told him what a comfort
In Memoriam had been to me, which pleased him, but he said I could
not believe the number of shameful letters of abuse he had received
about it. Incredible! When I took leave of him, I thanked him for his
kindness, and said I needed it . . . and he said, "You are so alone on
that terrible height; it is terrible. I've only a year or two to live, but
I shall be happy to do anything for you I can. Send for me whenever
you like!".'

There is fire in Tennyson's answer to her letter of thanks, which
reveals the fervent tone of their meeting better than the straightforward style of the journal.

'Dear and Honoured Lady,

MY QUEEN

'Your Majesty's letter made me glad that even in so small a
matter I may have been of some service to you. I will not say that
"I am loyal", or that "Your Majesty is gracious", for these are old
hackneyed terms used and abused by every courtier, but I will say
that during our conversation, I felt the touch of that true friendship
which binds human beings together, whether they be kings or
cobblers . . . So it is that in spite of the loneliness of the throne and
Your Majesty's many losses, and this latest of your faithful servant,
the return of your beloved daughter (Beatrice) may be of some
solace to you.'

The Bard declared himself to be 'always' his Queen's 'affectionate servant'. He had to wait two years to the month before she ceased to be his 'very truly' and became his 'affectionately, V.R.I.' Tennyson suggested some lines for one of the memorial tablets to John Brown, and the Queen was so full of gratitude that in the September he was offered a peerage through his dear friend Mr Gladstone, who was then Prime Minister. The effort to persuade Tennyson to accept a peerage must have been the only occasion in their lives when the Queen and Gladstone worked together in amicable and earnest collusion, and perhaps it is surprising that their shared feelings of warmth and admiration for the Poet did not succeed in bettering their relations through the years.

The Queen, when writing to Tennyson to assure him of her pleasure that he had accepted his peerage, did not find a congratulatory note an unsuitable organ for complaining to such a friend about a nuisance which she still took much to heart.

'How I wish,' she added, 'you could suggest means of crushing those horrible publications whose object is to promulgate scandal and calumny which they invite themselves!'

Henceforth, until his death, the seventy-four-year-old Laureate had the additional duty of confidant of the Queen's family worries and sorrows. One subdued little note of the Queen's sent in the spring of 1874 with a newly published copy of *Further Leaves from Our Life in the Highlands*, adopted a tone which few who had dealings with the Queen would have found unfamiliar.

'Dear Lord Tennyson,
'Though a very humble and unpretending author I send you my new book, which perhaps you may like to glance at. Its only merit is its simplicity and truth.
'What a warm winter we have had!
           Ever yours truly, V.R.I.'

When Princess Beatrice was to be married at Osborne in the summer of 1875 to Prince Henry of Battenberg, the Queen invited

her Laureate to the wedding. He was seventy-seven, and declined –
'I think that, blind as I am, growing blinder, I am best away from
the wedding' – but he sat down at his untidy desk and wrote the
Princess a suitable poem, of which he ordered one hundred copies
to be sent to Osborne.

From the happy words of the Queen at the period of the wedding
it might have seemed that the arrangement was a thing of delight
and satisfaction to her; but if such was the case the development was
a recent one caused by her discovery that the bride and bridegroom
were willing to devote their lives to her and travel with her from
place to place.

The Queen had always liked handsome, bearded young Henry
of Battenberg, and found him entertaining. His family was excellent;
he had a German military background; his bachelor life was without
aim or prospect, and he was reasonably frugal by necessity. Yet when
Beatrice came to tell her that at last she had found a man she could
love and that he was Henry of Battenberg, the Queen was not ready
to commit herself. Her daughter's confession of her love was greeted
with tears and a threat of speechless collapse; even when the Queen
still refused to speak to her next day, although she seemed to expect
her more or less constant presence, nobody surmised what was in the
wind.

For the next six months mother and daughter followed their
intimate daily lives together. Only one item of their partnership was
abnormal: they never spoke. They silently faced one another across
the breakfast table. A glum nod of greeting from the mother was
returned with a faint genuflexion by the daughter. After that their
gaze wandered from the table to objects round the room. During a
pause the firm but pudgy little hand of the Queen pushed a letter
over the table to Beatrice. It contained her plans and sundry directions for the day, which her daughter accepted with a hopeless little
smile, sometimes dropping her eyes if she caught her mother brush-
ing away a tear in the bitterness of estrangement. Dickens would have
appreciated the scene; but it would have painfully bewildered the
Bard of Farringford. When the Queen drove out in the afternoon

Beatrice sat beside her, always attentive to her needs, always listening for a word in case her mother forgot herself.

When six months had expired the Queen asked Beatrice if she still wished to marry Henry of Battenberg, now that she had been given time to think the matter over carefully without interference.

Beatrice replied that she did – but, of course, she would not think of letting marriage interrupt her happy companionship with her mother. She and Henry would always want to live with her and look after her. With a sunny smile the Queen gave Beatrice her blessing.

Marriage, even as Queen Victoria's resident son-in-law, was an answer to Henry of Battenberg's problems; moreover, he genuinely loved Beatrice. He agreed to the proposition, and although he had to suffer a good deal of scorn and criticism from the British, it was presently discovered that he was neither so tame nor so unscrupulous as some at first suspected; and that his influence with his mother-in-law, who soon had complete confidence in him, enabled him to be very useful on a number of occasions when others shrunk back.

The family wedding was to be at Whippenham Church – 'our village church' – and the Queen having accepted Tennyson's refusal to be present kept him posted about the details.

'... You may also like to know that she (Beatrice) will be followed by her ten nieces as bridesmaids, my eldest son's three girls, Louise, Victoria and Maud of Wales, dear Alice's two motherless girls, Irene and Alice of Hesse, Princess Christian's two, Victoria and Louise of Holstein, and my son Alfred's three, Marie, Victoria, and Alexandra Marie of Edinburgh.'

Then came 6 August, the Wedding Day, and the Queen's children and grandchildren, her sons-in-law and daughters-in-law, her nephews and nieces and German relations, crowded into Whippenham village in a blaze of finery and the musty church, stifling in the warm scent of flowers, was alive with guttural whisperings, and rustling silks.

Few but the dazzled villagers took much notice of the royal

wedding. The Press was terse and a little cruel. The Queen supplied her Laureate with one vivid paragraph.

'I wish you could have *seen* the wedding, for every one says it was the prettiest they ever saw. The simple, pretty little village church, all decorated with flowers, the sweet young bride, the handsome young husband, the ten bridesmaids, six of them quite children with flowing fair hair, the brilliant sunshine and the blue sea, all made up pictures not to be forgotten.

'Believe me always yours affectionately, V.R.I.'

PART FIVE

Fifty Years a Queen

11

Life with the Great White Goddess

THE popular glories and triumphs of 21 June, Jubilee Day, do not come within the compass of this personal study of Queen Victoria; but one scene of that tremendous day, witnessed by a comparative few, shall have its place because it must have been the best remembered moment by the Queen herself.

In Westminster Abbey the Thanksgiving Service had reached its end. The Queen sat on her throne, tiny and round, black and white, flashing with jewels. Caught in a bright shaft of sunlight slanting from a window, encircling her in a pale miasma of dancing dust particles, it almost seemed as if the Queen had reached the Olympian Mists.

At the back of the throne on chairs sat the great array of her family: the princes of the first generation on the right, the princesses on the left; and between them the grandsons and granddaughters. Every princess, young or old, wore a gown of pale blue and white, and the eye was caught by the gleam of long golden hair.

All rose, standing very still with their eyes fixed on the back of the throne and its invisible occupant. Then at a signal there came a stir among them, and the head of a procession led by small granddaughters in single file moved out from the back of the throne and passed into the pool of sunlight round the Queen. Each of them came to the Queen and she gave them a kiss and a warm embrace. The organ pealed a march and they came on and on with increasing stature till the whole regiment of her progeny passed away into the shadows. Foreign representatives who watched the scene went home to spread the legend of the Royal Grandmother of Europe.

Probably the most symbolic surviving relic of Queen Victoria in the latter half of the eighties is a photograph taken in the drawing-room at Osborne in January 1888.

The Queen had begun to be absorbed in private theatricals in which she employed herself to a large extent as producer. But the *tableau vivants* performed by young Ladies of her suite, which the photograph depicts, was, one imagines, an amusing surprise for her. The scene displayed suggests the elaborate set-piece crowning a wedding cake. A small white platform, one step on another, is draped with wandering trails of greenery set with flowers. On a pedestal at the top rises a life-size bust of the Queen under her miniature crown. Five Ladies in white classical draperies adorn the platform. One stands on the left of the topmost plinth, painfully raising her arm aloft holding some object above the bust. Another kneels on the right, offering a wreath of adoration. Three more recline on the lower step in attitudes of reverential guardianship.

But if the Queen was content to enjoy the higher flattery, she was not conceited in the way of most women. Lord Esher tells of a photographic portrait of her, widely circulated and hastily engraved at the time of the Jubilee. The picture portrayed her making a kind of humorous grimace, which made her look a veritable Mrs Brown or Mrs Jones at the moment of emerging from the local. This so shocked and disgusted the whole family that they urged her to order it to be suppressed. The Queen met their indignation with amusement.

'Well, really,' she remarked, 'I think it's *very like!* I have *no* illusions about my personal appearance.'

Although her arrogance in relation to her Queenly office had always been disturbingly elevated, and had reached colossal proportions by the time of the Jubilee years, she seems to have manifested it in her personal life only whenever it was useful to her ends – which admittedly in her case was most of the time. But occasionally something happened which suggested that she was not at heart a being with much self-pride. Loss of face, for instance, such as some clumsy, ridiculous accident which can so sadly ruffle the pompous immaculacy of great persons, could wring from her a chuckle rather than angry embarrassment.

An example of this occurred at one of her Jubilee Drawing Rooms, at which tiresome functions she had begun to linger much longer than of old; apparently with enjoyment. As usual the room was packed and stifling and every eye was on the Queen. The white column of beplumed ladies filed breathlessly before her. The Duchess of Buccleugh, the Mistress of the Robes, thinking that the moment had come when the Queen needed 'straightening' put up her hands for this purpose. The Queen moved and the Duchess struck a smart blow against the miniature diamond crown attached to her sweeping head veil. The Crown and the veil ripped away from the Queen's head. The most intimate members of the suite never saw her without a white cap; but suddenly a great crowd was staring at a very *bourgeoise* old lady with some straggling sprouts of grey hair. In horror they gazed at the floor. The Queen examined the assembly with a faint smile, standing motionless and totally unperturbed while the trembling fingers of the Mistress of the Robes replaced her headgear.

Princess Marie-Louise, the youngest daughter of Princess Helena and Prince Christian, was fifteen when she attended her first dinner party with her grandmother at Balmoral in Jubilee year. Marie Louise sat next to the Lord Chancellor and never spoke. Suddenly the sepulchral voice of a footman murmured in her ear – 'The Queen wishes the young Princesses to remember that their duty is to entertain their neighbours at dinner.' She recalls that always after that she used to work out a series of remarks and rehearse these before coming down for Queen's Dinner.

In June of Jubilee year a new Bishop was promoted to the See of Winchester, and the Ceremony of the Homage before the Queen at Osborne gave rise to an amusing irregularity. The Home Secretary, or Under-Secretary, was expected to attend this solemn event. Lord Knutsford, the Under-Secretary, was sent down on this occasion, and having never before officiated at such a ceremony he did not know that he was supposed to bring with him *The Bishop's*

Homage, a lengthy printed document which was kept in a box at the Home Office.

A new Bishop when he offers his Homage kneels before the Sovereign with hands touching like one praying, and the Sovereign lays hands over his while he reads the long Homage, which is held before him.

Knutsford discovered his mistake soon after arrival. It was terrifying; but he was a man of resource. Soon, he would have to face an indignant Queen and a dismayed Bishop. He telegraphed to his secretary in Whitehall, ordering him to take the Homage from its box and telegraph it with the greatest care to Osborne. The hour appointed for The Homage arrived; so also did the Bishop of Winchester in the drawing-room, followed shortly afterwards by the Queen. Just at that moment it was whispered to Knutsford that the Homage had begun to come through from the Home Office. That was bound to take up some time.

An uneasy atmosphere reigned in the drawing-room. The Queen was beginning to look puzzled and restless as she eyed the Bishop impatiently, as if he was responsible for keeping her waiting. At last Knutsford decided that the time had come when he must confess his crime to the Queen. He had scarcely finished his explanation when she interrupted him:

'Well, don't waste time,' she snapped briskly, 'I can't wait long. It's quite unnecessary for the clerk to make a fair copy of the Homage! Tell him to send up the telegraph forms.'

A handful of rather crumpled forms was delivered to the drawing-room. The Bishop went on his knees and the Queen almost slapped her hands over his. He began to read the Homage in steady tones, but was much agitated and scarcely knew what he was reading. This accounted for an unfortunate slip at the end. Unhappily the secretary in London had not been quite sure that he had found the whole of the Homage in the box. The final words should have run, '*God Bless Queen Victoria*', but the Bishop of Winchester read what the secretary had written – '*God Bless Queen Victoria, there is nothing else in the box*'.

While on the subject of the Queen and her Bishops an incident, which also happened in Jubilee year, is recalled by Princess Marie Louise.

The Queen, immediately after receiving a large body of Bishops and High Church dignitaries at Windsor, took a drive in Windsor Park with Edith, Lady Lytton, who was in Waiting. They had driven off in silence and had reached the wide spaces of the Park when suddenly the Queen gave tongue.

'—A very Ugly Party!' she announced in firm tones.

The Lady-in-Waiting said nothing: she was startled and not absolutely sure that she had heard aright. A long pause followed: then the Queen spoke again:

'—I do NOT like Bishops!'

Lady Lytton stared at her in shocked surprise and felt moved to protest.

'Oh, but your dear Majesty likes *some* Bishops,' she cried, '—what about Randall-Davidson and Boyd-Carpenter of Ripon?'

'Yes,' agreed the Queen, 'I like the *Man* – but not the Bishop!'

When Chief Agbosome of the Gold Coast was brought down to Windsor to be privately presented to the Queen, she asked him what he would like best as a memento of their meeting. The Chief did not hesitate an instant when her words had been translated to him. His dark eyes flamed with eagerness and, pointing at her cap, he broke into a torrent of speech. The Queen stepped back and listened with a nervous smile.

Translated, Chief Agbosombe's declaration was that he wished for a widow's bonnet such as the 'Mighty Queen' wore – 'Give ME alone the right to wear it, and this pass to my successors!'

The Queen solemnly agreed to grant his line the sole right to wear her cap and ordered one to be delivered to him. Until recently the Chieftains sitting on the royal Stool of Agbosombe have worn Queen Victoria's cap or a replica of it.

A close friend of the Queen's, and a frequent guest in the royal homes, was the Empress Eugenie. The Queen had long adored the French Empress for her vivacious loveliness and grace and her wonderful dress-sense; and Eugenie had worshipped her with a touch of trepidation because of her terrifying Queenliness. When the Prince Imperial had been killed in Zululand the Queen had hurried down from Scotland to Chislehurst to comfort her – even to apologize for the base betrayal of her son by the British army – and was said thereby to have saved her from mental collapse. Since then the bond between them had been deep. Young Marie Louise was witness of a moving scene during a visit of the Empress to Windsor at this time.

The Princess, following her grandmother's orders, went to meet Empress Eugenie, who was coming from her apartments with her Lady-in-Waiting. She led them into the famous corridor; and there the Queen presently joined them.

The two elderly Sovereigns curtseyed and kissed, and then side-by-side reached the door of the dining-room. There they hesitated, faced each other and smiled:

'—*Apres vous, ma chère sœur,*' invited the Queen.

'—*Mais non, ma chère sœur, apres vous!*' deprecated the Empress.

Marie Louise recalls the picture: 'They bowed and curtseyed; then hand in hand these two old ladies went into lunch together. I followed in their wake. It was just a tiny silhouette of court etiquette of long ago.'

Young people were beginning to find the Queen fascinating; and the unpredictability of the ideas she expressed endeared her to them. Not one of them wanted to defy her openly; although at times she was a nuisance. They spoke of her in terms which today seem positively fulsome. She really seems in her later years to have somehow acquired the ability to make the young feel she understood and sympathized with them.

Princess Marie Louise and her sister once wanted to play tennis on a Sunday afternoon at Balmoral. They did not think the Queen would mind, as she was not 'stuffy' about things of that kind; but everything which happened at the Castle had to be referred to her.

Grandmama's reply was unexpected in some respects.

'Yes, you can play,' she nodded, 'so long as you pick up the balls yourselves. Being Sunday I don't think it right to make others work for you.'

But if the young did not openly go against some of the Queen's theories, Henry Ponsonby shows that they had ways of deceiving her; and in the case he depicts some quite mature people, including her own children, connived at the deceit. The eighties and nineties had a cycle of cold winters and as a result open-air skating was a popular pastime of the period. Very frequently at Osborne the big pond near Barton Manor was frozen hard, and the princesses and the household would go out to skate. The Queen usually passed that way on her afternoon drive, and it was her custom to stop and watch the figure-skating, which amused her.

In those days everybody carried walking-sticks in the country, and somebody always brought a cork ice-hockey ball down to the pond. This was a favourite pastime and the Ladies were as keen about it as the men. To this the Queen strongly objected, especially if her daughters or granddaughters took part, because the Ladies in their long petticoats, however skilled they were at ordinary skating, were quite likely to take an indelicate tumble in an unrestrained set-to at ice-hockey.

Directly the Queen's outrider appeared over the crest of the hill, all the players hurled their sticks on to the bank and pocketed the ball. When the carriage appeared the party were earnestly employed in figure-skating, and thanks to the outrider the Queen never discovered that her veto on Ladies' ice-hockey was disobeyed for years.

The near divine status of the Queen did not deter the public from writing to her. Her public mail increased. People were eager to try their hand at consulting the Oracle; but only a selection went up for her personal reply. She did not always approve of the choice, and her answer sometimes needed to have the bluntness chiselled off it before posting.

When, in 1888, Oscar Wilde wrote to say that he wished to make a record of poems written by the Queen in her girlhood she was not amused.

'Really, what will people not say and invent,' she scribbled.

'Never could the Queen in her whole life write *one line of poetry* serious or comic or make a Rhyme even.'

She had not much sympathy with writers, for like her eldest son, she could rarely manage to reach half-way through a book, but she liked to pretend that she read everything fashionable. She used to interrogate her Ladies about new publications, and afterwards talked about these with such an air of authority that she even fooled people not in the know.

The Queen could be most considerate to correspondents; and a certain Miss Low, who was writing a book on historic dolls and wished to know if the Queen had played with dolls as a child, was probably well pleased with her answer:

'The Queen has no hesitation in saying that she was quite devoted to dolls and played with them till she was fourteen. Her favourites were small ones and small wooden ones which could be dressed as she liked and had a house. None of her children loved them as she did – but then she was an only child and except for occasional visits of other children lived always *alone*, without companions.'

The letter is perhaps important in its way, as showing the child from which Queen Victoria developed. As for her dolls; after lying scattered in confusion in the deserted royal apartments of Kensington Palace for more than half a century, these were collected by Lord Esher in 1900 and, with the Queen's approval, exhibited in a glass case, where they still remain.

The revived royal ardour for theatricals began with the organization of *tableau vivants*, and went on from these to plays performed by the household, and finally to visits to the royal homes by London professionals.

The producer of the Queen's plays was usually the Hon. Alec Yorke, a jaunty and very much favoured young Groom-in-Waiting. The Queen liked to choose the play, attend all rehearsals, cut or totally alter the script to suit her taste, tell the actors and actresses how they were to act with demonstrations by herself, supervise their costumes and the making of the scenery. Her delight was childish. She knew the play by heart before it came to performance;

and sometimes she was the only person who did so, owing to the numerous interpolations she had added during rehearsal. Matters of State came secondary to the play in hand. The Private Secretary would rise with a sigh from his crowded desk in the office in mid-morning to rehearse his part, slip away to resume national business as soon as he could, and rejoin the company when the Queen sent for him. The princesses and their husbands – or possibly the elder grandchildren – were required for the spectacular roles, as the Queen hardly thought it suitable that anyone of the household should outshine them.

The most ambitious play ever put on was *She Stoops to Conquer*, at Osborne. It was notable among other things for the appearance of three Ponsonbys in the cast: Sir Henry and two of his sons, Arthur and Frederick; the latter of whom was shortly to begin his career under the Queen in somewhat unexpected and dramatic circumstances.

Frederick Ponsonby, who had seen little of the Queen previously and was very much frightened by her presence in the auditorium, was destined when he first entered royal service to distinguish himself by a series of unhappy *faux-pas*. He committed one on this occasion when he first aroused her interest. Frederick had to use some light badinage with Princess Louise, whose part required her to pose as a barmaid; and in nervous excitement he chucked her very intimately under the chin. A note from the Queen was handed to him. It said that the Queen thought he had *better not* chuck the Princess under the chin.

Next day he went through his performance without touching Princess Louise. He felt it was rather spiritless; so did the Queen. She sent him up a note: Could he not put more life into his acting? After all, the scene was intended to be lively.

He went to Princess Louise and told her he was in trouble. After much laughter they arranged some business between them which satisfied the Queen.

In her youth the Queen had been so passionate a lover of the theatre that she had all but torn down the curtains of the royal box in her excitement; but after the Consort's death no professional theatrical performance came her way until 1889, when Henry Irving, invited by the Prince of Wales, brought down his famous Lyceum company to Sandringham during the Queen's visit.

Irving, then the unrivalled King of the London theatre world, considered this event a landmark in stage history. Always the enthusiast rather than the businessman, he cancelled his Lyceum performances for three nights, paid the salaries of his cast himself, and also paid for the making of miniature sets of the elaborate stage scenery he always insisted upon. Thus, 'the Guv'nor', as he was affectionately called, was heavily out of pocket.

There could be no doubt that he curdled the royal blood by his celebrated performance of *The Bells*, and followed this by another of his favourites; the Trial Scene from *The Merchant of Venice*.

The Queen was not used to this new, realistic style of acting; and at the end of *The Bells* – said to be the most terrifying and shattering dramatic piece within living memory – appeared dazed and dumbfounded, if not affronted. She had ordered that spectators were to applaud as they thought fit; but as she herself had feebly applauded the others observed a sympathetic restraint.

The Merchant of Venice was more to her taste; although the violence of Irving as 'Shylock' was inclined to be overpowering.

The Queen was still overwhelmed and hesitant when Irving and Ellen Terry were afterwards brought up to be introduced; and scarcely did more than nod graciously to them. She had never seen any actor like Henry Irving. He was the caricature of all actors: a giant towering over her, with a black mop of hair elegantly flounced around his collar and dense black beetling eyebrows frowning above piercing eyes. His rich, sonorous, booming voice was that night thick with nervous incoherence as he hovered over the little Queen. But the royal graciousness was sufficient to send 'the Guv'nor' into an ecstasy of patriotic reverence.

The next time the Queen saw Irving and Ellen Terry was in the Waterloo Chamber at Windsor when they performed Tennyson's *Becket*. This was a much more elaborate production – and 'the

Guv'nor' had paid for it all. But his reward was more than ample. The Queen was observed chatting amiably with him and Ellen Terry after the performance.

'It is a very noble play,' she was heard to assure him. 'What a pity old Tennyson did not live to see it. It would have delighted him as it has delighted Us!'

She wrote about it in her journal:'—The performance was over by twelve and we went to the drawing-room, all the visitors passing by, after which Irving and Ellen Terry came in. I spoke to them and told them how pleased I was. She is very tall, pleasing and ladylike.'

It had been a thrilling evening, and the Queen, much to the astonishment of the household, signified her enjoyment by permitting Mr Bram Stoker, Irving's irrepressible Irish manager and author of the world-famous *Dracula*, to telegraph a detailed report of the event to the Press from the Castle post-office. That in itself made stage history.

The fascinating Ellen Terry, famed for the most beautiful of stage voices, coined a description of the royal voice which is probably the finest ever thought of:

'Queen Victoria's voice,' she declared, 'was like a silver stream flowing over golden stones.'

Three years after *Becket*, Henry Irving received the coveted award which was to make his profession respectable. The Queen summoned him to Windsor to receive the first stage of knighthood – and this he saw not as an accolade for all that he himself had done for the stage, but as an honourable recognition of the people with whom he had spent his life.

As the royal swordpoint touched the shoulder upon which the wavy hair of the great actor almost rested, the Queen was heard to break her unvarying rule of saying only the traditional words as the new knight knelt before her. Her clear voice carried though the room:

'—I am so glad – I am so very glad!' she told him.

In 1888 the Queen elected to spend her continental holiday at

Biarritz, then becoming highly fashionable, and her choice of residence involved her Private Secretary in a comically dramatic embarrassment.

The Queen had accepted the offer of the *Villa La Ravillion* from the Comte de la Rochefoucauld who, although she had not his acquaintance, had begged to place it at her disposal. The Comtesse de La Rochefoucauld was by her marriage entitled to think herself one of the most distinguished of French aristocrats, although she was by birth an Englishwoman who had been divorced from an English husband in scandalous circumstances.

This would not have mattered in the least if the de La Rochefoucaulds had not, upon vacating their villa for the Queen, moved into another house in Biarritz. The Comtesse, of course, by virtue of her past record, must in no circumstances be allowed to come near the Queen. The Comte, on the other hand, as one of the leading fashionables of the resort could, and probably would, pay his respects to her.

The whole circumstances of the case were known to Henry Ponsonby, and he thought it wisest, in order to save hurt feelings in Biarritz, to write to the Comtesse, explaining as politely as possible that Court etiquette ruled that she must not appear in the Queen's presence. The Comtesse answered his letter in a rather less frigid tone than he had expected, and he did not feel she was entirely convinced by his words of the seriousness of the matter. Among other things she remarked that she could not see the justice of this royal veto being applied to her; as her ex-husband was dead and had in any case, as she could prove, been a very bad man. The Private Secretary wrote again a good deal more forcibly, but still preserving a blandness which he later regretted.

Upon the arrival of the royal party at Biarritz, and while the Queen was being welcomed by the municipality, Henry Ponsonby hired a cab and drove off to the *Villa La Revillion*. He had heard that the Comte de La Rochefoucauld was waiting to welcome the Queen on the porch of the villa, and that he had a golden key which he was going to present to her. That being the case it was as well that the Private Secretary should precede the Queen and see that things were so arranged as not to cause her annoyance.

A gay and splendidly dressed group of men, women and children, clutching flowers, stood chattering excitedly on the doorstep as he alighted from the cab outside the big, white, sunlit villa. The Comte and Comtesse stood beaming before the family party. The Comtesse rushed forward and caught the Private Secretary by both hands.

'Tell us – how should the Queen be received?' she cried breathlessly.

For a moment his brain reeled. There were only a few minutes to spare.

At last he said, '—By the Comte alone – Comtesse!'

His voice had been firm, and she looked at him steadily; then she smiled:

'—Oh, may I stand behind the front door?' she pleaded.

He had not the heart to refuse so pathetic a request from a beautiful woman.

'If the Comte alone receives the Queen, and you stand in the recess,' he muttered urgently, '—that will do—' He could hear the crunching of wheels on gravel and knew the Queen's carriages were arriving.

The Queen accepted the golden key from the Comte, and greeted the party less amiably than she might have done. Then, with an almost audible sigh of relief, she mounted the steps. The Comtesse burst from the recess and thrust a large bouquet into her hands. Then she curtseyed, recoiled, and embraced the Queen's Ladies one by one, causing confusion on the steps. The Queen observed her with grim astonishment and walked on into the hall.

'H.M. sent for me afterwards and was very indignant,' Ponsonby told his wife: 'But what could be done: Nothing.'

At that point he felt no doubt that was an end of the matter.

The next move was that the Comte made friends with Prince Henry of Battenberg in the Casino. Prince Henry was very sorry for the Comtesse. His influence with the Queen was already considerable and he promised to take up the subject with her. The Queen said that if the Comtesse had been divorced, then there was no case to be argued. When this was known dismay reigned in the home of the Comte and Comtesse. It was not long before the lady found that the Comte was to blame: he had caused her to be divorced; he was a weakling and an idiot; why was he not protecting her honour?

The Comte de La Rochefoucauld arrived in the Private Secretary's Office, and it was so evident from his ravaged aspect that he had fled from a desperate scene, that Ponsonby knew a 'terrible interview' was about to begin.

The Comte started to plead his wife's cause. He was almost on his knees; his hands appeared to be raised in supplication; tears streamed over his cheeks. He kept running up and down, storming, shouting, quite demented, and he must have been audible all over the villa. He was threatening the Private Secretary – and even the Queen – with the horrors of the Law! Henry Ponsonby thought he was about to be challenged to a duel. and wondered whether he would be more clumsy with sword or pistol. As Private Secretary he would have to face even that on the Queen's behalf.

An hour had passed. The Comte was still striding round the Secretary's table biting his lips: suddenly he glared at Ponsonby and roared, '—Do you hear – even the good God himself thinks twice before insulting a de La Rochefoucauld!' Like a flash he rushed from the office and vanished down the drive.

For several days Ponsonby expected the Comte's seconds to call upon him; but they never appeared. Instead a parcel arrived addressed to the Private Secretary. Inside was an 'immense packet of letters', which were intended to prove how cruelly the Comtesse had been used by her late husband. These were to be read by the Queen, who must then surely see things in a different light. There does seem some reason for supposing that the kind-hearted Henry Ponsonby, not unmoved by this, did try to make the Queen reconsider the Comtesse's case. If that was so, doubtless a stern note which the Queen sent him nerved him to face any further de La Rochefoucauld overtures with adamantine firmness.

'—The de La Rochefoucaulds are quite intolerable. The Queen

will not see her on any account and if she forces herself forward the Queen will not look at her.'

So far as the Queen was concerned that was the end of the de La Rochefoucauld affair; but to the household the Comte and Comtesse were still a power to be reckoned with. Indeed, they were a nightmare. Any member of the suite who ventured from the grounds of the villa was liable to be rushed upon by the Comte or the Comtesse, in the street, in the Casino, on the Plage, where the tussle was renewed before an interested audience. Continental holidays were never very happy events for the Queen's attendants; but the shadow of the de La Rochefoucaulds was said to have made this one the grimmest on record.

12

The Triumph of Abdul the Munshi

SHORTLY after John Brown had died, and while not a few were
expressing their satisfaction that he would be met with no more
in the royal homes Sir Francis Knollys, Secretary to the Prince
of Wales, wrote to his friend Henry Ponsonby. He held views concerning the demise of Brown which at the time sounded exaggerated;
but which were to prove grimly prophetic:

'I have for a long time been one of those who had thought that if
anything happened to him (Brown) worse might happen,' suggested
Sir Francis. '—I mean in this way that his successor might do a deal
more harm that Brown. If he had been an ambitious man . . . I
presume all the family will rejoice at his death, but I think very
probably they are shortsighted.'

As Jubilee year approached it had been suggested to the Queen
that the people of India would be much pleased if she henceforth had
a number of picked Indian servants or Khirmutgars, who would
attend her at all times. She agreed with enthusiasm, and declared also
that she would like to learn Hindustani. The Khirmutgars arrived
at Balmoral in 1887, and one of the Extra-Grooms-in-Waiting,
Major General Dennehy, late of the Rajputana political service, was
put in charge of them. The Queen talked excitedly about her new
acquisitions, and told everybody that they must follow her example
and learn Hindustani. She could be seen studying the Khidmutgars
with uninhibited admiration; and they were certainly an impressive
addition to the majesty of the Presence – tall, thickly-bearded men
in large turbans and long-coated white or scarlet liveries with
embroidered breast insignias and broad sashes. The Queen was never
seen unescorted by one of them. Her Khirmutgar stood behind her

chair at meals, beside her desk in the Closet, where he held her walking-stick held across his body like a soldier's rifle; and she quickly learnt to take his arm for support as she moved about on her rheumatic legs. She gave the Private Secretary a Hindu dictionary – which he was too busy to open. Her Indians were dolls; toys who gave her daily pleasure as they glided about in noiseless reverence. The household were amused; deciding that she was rather more easy to deal with than before.

That Christmas at Windsor people remarked that it was plain the Queen had a favourite among the Khirmutgars. His name was Abdul Karim, and he was a Moslem. His English was better than that of the other Khidmutgars and the Queen kept holding long conversations with him. His once statuesque poses while on duty grew careless; his face, no longer a bearded mask, twitched with knowing alertness. In the early months of the coming year complaints were heard that Abdul Karim was insolent; and more than one member of the household revealed their annoyance to General Dennehy. The General shrugged his shoulders, saying that there was nothing he could do because the Queen obviously approved of the man. Abdul Karim was in one respect different from his fellow Khidmutgars: in India he had been not a professional servant but a clerk. Perhaps it had been suggested to him that if he could engage himself as a Queen's Khirmutgar he might in due course get himself promoted to Queen's Munshi, or teacher of Hindustani. He had had ample opportunities of telling the Queen about himself, and was finding in her an eager listener; even if everybody else at Court treated him as a piece of furniture.

In the autumn of 1888 the Queen told Henry Ponsonby, who still combined the duties of Privy Purse with that of Secretary, that Abdul Karim had informed her that his father was a Surgeon-General of the Indian Medical Service. He should never have been put on domestic duties and was to be taken off them and out of livery. His pay was to be increased and he was to be given the title of Munshi Hafez Abdul Karim, the Queen's teacher of Hindustani. When on duty he was to wear a frockcoat like the other Gentlemen, but she wished him to retain the turban. She also said that she had found him a most intelligent man, and that he would be very useful to her as an unofficial secretary and adviser when she dealt with Indian affairs.

News of this was a bombshell to the household. Those who had served in India asserted that by certain mannerisms, they were sure Abdul Karim had been born of the servant class, even if he had become a clerk. If the Queen had not been in her sixty-ninth year there would, even before the elevation of Abdul Karim to 'Munshi', have been an outbreak of the same kind of scandalous whispering and horrified insinuation as had followed upon the advent of John Brown. People had found it more difficult to take the signs seriously, although it was plain to see that the Queen doted on this liveried Indian and treated him with a familiarity never used toward a servant in that country. From then on, Abdul Karim was always referred to in a cool tone as 'the Munshi'. Since he could be relied upon to return coolness by rudeness, he was avoided as much as possible; which could still be managed as he lived a somewhat lonely life when the Queen did not call for his company.

Early in 1890 a theatrical entertainment was arranged to take place in the Waterloo Gallery. All the household, including the upper and lower servants, were expected to attend. When the Munshi entered he was shown to the row in which the Queen's dressers were sitting. These elegant ladies, who conducted themselves with considerable exclusiveness because they were reputed to wield much influence with Her Majesty, were about to be shocked and insulted. The Munshi, instead of taking his seat, stood glaring at them. He broke into high-pitched English, whereat everybody turned round:

'—This is not the place to send the son of a Surgeon-General in the Indian Medical Service!' he expostulated.

An argument started with stewards; all equally indignant. Angry servants behind him and angry gentlemen in front told him to sit down. Voices rose, and as the commotion grew, members of the family and other royal guests in the front rows, looked nervously towards the door through which the Queen was expected at any moment. Just before she appeared Abdul Karim stalked dramatically from the hall: he did not return.

When the Queen heard of this she expressed her indignation against the official who had allotted the Munshi such a humiliating seat. Further to emphasize her point she gave instructions that Abdul Karim, being an Indian gentleman, had a right to join the Gentlemen in the household billiard-room when she had retired for the night; also that he was to attend the Household Dinner whenever he wished to do so.

Few Indian princelings were very acceptable in those days; and it was doubted if the Munshi was even a *gentleman*. The first time he appeared in the doorway of the household billiard-room and nonchalantly lit a cigar, those Gentlemen who had Indian experience were seized by such a blind sense of outrage that their amused companions could scarcely restrain them from throwing him out. Fuel was added to the flames when the story got about that the Queen, at the Munshi's request, had ordered all photographs which showed him waiting at table, or performing other servile duties, to be collected and destroyed. The story happened to be true. Shortly afterwards, the Munshi came for the first time to a Household Dinner.

Nobody could complain of his manners – he had experienced plenty of opportunities for studying table etiquette – and since none of the diners of either sex seemed inclined to talk that night, the Munshi had a free field to boast of his many intimate conversations with Her Majesty: a privilege which few others present had ever enjoyed. After dinner, while the household propped themselves against the walls in the royal corridor waiting for the Queen to address an occasional word to them, the Munshi stood beside her chair, bending with an intimate smile to hand her objects off her little table, and as chief recipient of her observations whispering his replies in her ear as he eyed his fellow courtiers with mild disdain. It was probably due entirely to the tact and influence of Henry Ponsonby, who was convinced nothing could be done with the Queen about Abdul Karim, that all the Ladies and Gentlemen, after a few words, agreed to wish the Munshi 'Good Morning' each day upon first encountering him.

During the Queen's stay in Scotland in the summer of 1890 she attended the Braemar gathering, and the tall turbaned figure of Munshi Hafez Abdul Karim, clad in fashionable and loud sporting outfit, was 'very conspicuous among the gentry'. Such was his dignity and style that many mistook him for some Indian Rajah much favoured by the Queen, and were impressed as he hovered about her or swaggered through the enclosure. Members of the family who were present were moved by very different feelings: they were furious and ashamed. The Duke of Connaught, familiar with India, could not contain himself. He fell upon Henry Ponsonby, addressing him in his most fiery military manner.

'—Something has got to be done about HIM!' he roared.

Ponsonby mildly assured him that the Munshi was there by the Queen's order:

'—I replied (to the Duke) that as I did not understand Indian etiquette, as H.R.H. did, would it not be better for him to mention it to the Queen. That entirely shut him up.'

So far it was generally believed that the learning of Hindustani constituted the main bond between the Queen and her Indian favourite. If she discussed Indian affairs with him this was not taken very seriously. The Queen usually referred to him as 'the dear Munshi', and as had been the case with Brown she often quoted his words or explained his feelings to other people. When she had first mooted her idea of using him as her Indian Secretary nothing had been thought of the matter. But as time went on 'the dear Munshi' was no longer a frequent phrase on the Queen's lips, and instead she would say with a look of pride, 'my Indian Secretary'. This title was especially exasperating to the Anglo-Indians,[1] who knew from having had so often to listen to Abdul Karim's monologues, that his views on the way things ought to be conducted in India were disgustingly liberal and advanced.

All documents, including those marked *Secret*, brought up to the

[1]As they were called in those days.

Queen in the Indian boxes became known to the Munshi, since he stood beside her, blotting her signature and ready to offer comments or suggestions. Then a new order was issued by the Queen: an office and English clerks were to be allotted to the Indian secretary: everything Indian which reached her hands would in future pass to his office before she set her signature to it. At first the Munshi's allotment of clerks was small; but gradually more appeared on the pay list and he tried to impress other colleagues by describing the increasing importance of his office. High officials of the India Office, who had never heard of Abdul Karim, came to visit the Queen to discuss confidential matters of the first importance and, seeing a strange Indian hovering in the Closet, assumed they must wait to get down to business till the Queen sent him away. They were startled when the Queen began to question them in his presence: in bewilderment they listened to Her Majesty consulting the Munshi over their heads; and heard him answer her with a blunt familiarity which sounded monstrously insolent when used by an Indian to his Queen Empress. They recounted their strange experience when they returned to the India Office.

At Osborne the Queen had a large bungalow built for the Munshi, and presented him with furniture, linen, carpets and curtains at considerable cost. It was presently observed that several Indian ladies had taken up residence at the bungalow. Some of these were plump and middle-aged; others younger and more strikingly clad in rich and brilliant saris. Seeing these saris spread out to dry on the verandah, passers-by recalled that Moslems had generous ideas about wives and concubines. The Munshi spoke of them all as his 'aunts'. One male Indian visitor aroused sharp curiosity, because he appeared to be the special friend and companion of the Munshi. This man was suave and highly educated; but something about him suggested that he was sinister.

A whisper went round that this mysterious Indian could be definitely identified with the anti-British underground, which had become gradually active in India since the collapse of the Mutiny. Even Arthur Bigge, the loyal Assistant Secretary who refrained

from pushing his own ideas, expressed his perturbation about the
Abdul Karim problem and urged Henry Ponsonby to do something.
Others had already passed hints on the matter. Everybody seemed
persuaded that it was up to the Private Secretary. Ponsonby wrote
despairingly to his wife that he thought he could deal pretty well
with English or European affairs, 'but these Injuns are too much for
me'.

So far as the royal family and the household were concerned the
Munshi was another John Brown, whom the Queen regarded as her
only true friend; although the Indian was so lacking in the coarser,
more spectacular, characteristics of the Scotsman that some who had
been the latter's bitterest detractors in life now referred to him
almost with nostalgia.

The Prince of Wales had inevitably come to hate the Munshi:
first from jealousy and mortification; later even more fiercely when
in addition his suspicions began to be aroused. Once an idea was put
into the Prince's head he invariably talked about it everywhere. He
pushed it like an able salesman, and as a result the London clubs and
dinner-tables were soon buzzing with the sinister scandal of the
Munshi. Was the Queen actually infatuated with an Indian traitor?
With the masses the story of the Munshi made little headway. It
lacked the warm human interest of the Brown scandal, and in any
case such a tale about the Great White Goddess was beyond belief.

Nevertheless, by the beginning of 1894 the newspapers both in
Britain and in India were taking an interest in the problem of the
Munshi. These did not insinuate that the Queen was harbouring a
traitor in her Indian favourite – that brand of journalism would have
been too risky around the *fin de siècle* – but they did strongly suggest
that the Munshi was an impudent impostor who was making a fool
of the aged Queen, and that it was wrong that he should be entrusted
with confidential matters of State.

The newspapers attacks caused the Queen to write in incoherent
indignation from Florence on 10 April 1894, to the Private Secretary,
ordering him not to let these influence him against Abdul Karim.

'—the poor dear Munshi – she would wish to observe that to

make out he is really so *low* is *outrageous*–he (Abdul) feels cut to the heart at being thus spoken of – the Queen is so sorry for the poor Munshi's feelings.'

Hitherto, the Ministers of the Crown had declined to take the affair of the Munshi as a very serious business; but eventually the continual loquacity of the Prince of Wales made them uneasy. On second thoughts, and unknown to the Queen, they sent instructions to the authorities in India to be on the alert and to furnish a report as to the possibility of leakages of information.

Whatever answer was anticipated to this inquiry in Whitehall, that which presently reached the India Office, sanctioned by the approval of the Viceroy, was of a character calculated to inflict a severe shock. The report stated that as a result of extensive investigation by the Intelligence, matters of the most confidential nature concerning the Government of India seemed often to have been known to the revolutionary elements throughout India – and sometimes even to the shopkeepers in the bazaars before documents and directives had left the India Office in London. In fact, the Viceroy might have gained first knowledge of policies he was expected to carry out from gossip in the backstreets of native quarters.

Since the India Office employed no Indians in confidential posts, the inference that the Munshi was the source of leakage seemed to be pretty conclusive.

But what was to be done? This aspect of the Munshi affair must be hushed up at all costs, or the most appalling national scandal might envelop the Throne – therefore the matter was kept secret. Even the Prince of Wales stopped talking when the gravity of the problem was brought home to him. But things could not be left there: the information must not be allowed to go on leaking.

Who was unwittingly responsible for this betrayal of secrets? The Queen – assuming that her Indian favourite was the culprit. SHE was the one being in the United Kingdom who, if concerned in such a transaction, could not be handled like anybody else. She could not be threatened. She could not be given orders. She could not be convinced about anything if she was determined not to be convinced, and she had ruses for stopping people broaching a second time any subject which she had dismissed at the first approach.

Often in human affairs problems seem to solve themselves untidily rather than submitting to a neat settlement by planned efforts; and something of this kind seems to have happened in the Munshi affair. According to Frederick Ponsonby, that son of Henry Ponsonby we have already met in Osborne theatricals, his father was not the one who at this crisis approached the Queen about the Munshi. Perhaps Henry Ponsonby declined the assignment, convinced that it was hopeless and that 'Injuns' were beyond him. His assistant, Arthur Bigge, who was to succeed him in 1895, backed by Major Fleetwood-Edwards and Sir James Reid, the Resident Physician who had followed in the sacred footprints of 'Jenner', were the trio who resolutely approached the Queen.

The nature of this stormy interview is only known by the results. When they emerged the Queen had defiantly assured them that to put a stop once and for all to this nonsense about the Munshi being an impostor, she herself would set afoot private inquiries in India which would establish his honour.

At this point Frederick Ponsonby came on the scene. He was on the eve of entry into royal service and that entry, thanks to Abdul Karim, was to be somewhat unfortunate. Frederick was a subaltern in the Grenadier Guards and was then serving as an A.D.C. to the Viceroy of India. Earlier in the year, without warning, he had received a telegram from the Queen offering him the vacant post of an Extra-Equerry. It was a great honour for so young a man; but having had theatrical experience of *H.M.* at Osborne he did not want it. The first his father had known about the Queen's offer – she had intended it as a delightful surprise for him – was a telegram from Frederick asking if he could possibly refuse the post. The answer had been NO, so he had accepted. During the summer and shortly before he was due to return home to go into Waiting, he received a telegram from the Queen ordering him to go to Agra and call upon the father of Munshi Hafez Abdul Karim.

Frederick Ponsonby had never heard of the Munshi and had no

idea why he was to make such a visit; but he took train to Agra and stayed with the O.C. Troops. Inquiries were set afoot for him in the city, and eventually he was directed to go to the Agra Jail. There an elderly Indian, who was the jail apothecary, admitted to being the father of the Queen's Munshi. He spoke only Hindustani, and was somewhat nervous of the officer-sahib, so that the conversation did not prosper as Frederick's knowledge of Hindustani was very limited. But he left the jail confident on one point: the apothecary had agreed that he was the father of the Queen's Munshi.

Frederick received no further communication from the Queen, and not having been commanded to render a report about his Agra visit, he sailed for home carrying with him the secret of Abdul Karim's parentage.

Soon after he arrived at Osborne House the Queen asked for her new Extra-Equerry to be brought to be presented to her. She greeted him warmly, saying how truly glad she was that a son of dear Sir Henry could come to serve her; but this phase of welcome was brief. She asked if he had been to Agra for her and called upon the father of Munshi Hafez Abdul Karim.

'Yes, Ma'am,' he answered casually. 'I had some difficulty in finding him as the information sent to me about him seems to have been wrong. I found him in the end at Agra Jail, where he is the apothecary.'

Frederick knew the Queen well enough to be puzzled by the pregnant silence which fell after his words, but was totally in the dark as to the shock he had dealt her.

'Impossible!' she exclaimed. 'There is a mistake. You must have visited the wrong person. That is what you evidently did—'

'No, Ma'am,' he assured her confidently, 'I'm quite sure this was the right person. He told me he was his father.'

The Queen signified that the interview was at an end, and Frederick Ponsonby bowed himself out, crestfallen and at a loss. The Queen did not speak to him again for more than twelve months.

They had not been alone when these words had passed; so that the truth about the Munshi's origins was out. The Queen's instincts were roused in defence of her favourite. She called upon her son-in-law Henry of Battenberg to rally to her cause. As a Court diplomat he had become much sought after, and many had found him very useful. He only knew Abdul Karim as the Queen's favourite. As a German he had not the prejudice against Indians which prevailed among the English courtiers. Whatever his personal feelings about the Munshi he could see no reason why the Queen at her age should not be allowed to have any personal attendant who could keep her happy. The slights he had seen given to the Indian had sometimes disgusted him.

Henry therefore expressed himself strongly on the Queen's side. This was exactly the backing she wanted to fortify her against her enemies in her intention to carry on as before in her association with the Munshi. As long as Henry of Battenberg stood by the Queen nothing could be done. He had to be made to alter his views, and the way to do this was to reveal to him the grave suspicions of treason held against him in Whitehall. Frederick Ponsonby says that this was done by putting in his hands a letter written by Lord George Hamilton, the Secretary of State for India. This letter declared that if confidential papers on Indian affairs were in future shown to the Munshi he would consider it his duty to refuse to submit all such documents to the Queen. Ponsonby does not state to whom this letter was addressed; but one thing is certain: had this ultimatum been presented to the Queen and had she defied it, a most dangerous crisis must have arisen and the Queen's insistence on harbouring an alleged traitor must have been exposed to the public. Some of the documents concerned needed the Queen's signature to become valid and by withholding these from her, Indian affairs would come to a standstill. The Government challenged by her might feel bound to resign, and it might well be that in the extraordinary circumstances it would have been impossible for her to find a new Ministry willing to serve her.

Henry of Battenberg, having digested these dire possibilities, agreed that the picture was entirely changed. He went to the Queen and said that from what he had been hearing the Hindus of India

were becoming restive through jealousy, because it was known to
them that the Queen was employing a Moslem as her confidential
secretary. He followed this up by declaring that her magnificently
loyal Indian princes, whom she always regarded with so much
esteem, were growing deeply perturbed because they could not help
feeling insulted that she was entrusting the most delicate problems
of their country to a person held in so little esteem in India as was
the Munshi.

The Queen gave her close attention to this. Her good sense made
her accept that it was probably true, or that it soon would be so.
Perhaps, also, she perceived that her son-in-law had offered her a
chance to save face. He had not suggested that she must give up the
Munshi; but only that he must not see confidential documents
which affected the government of India.

From that time onwards the Munshi fades into the Court background. The Queen continued to refer to him as her Indian Secretary: he persisted in keeping full to overflowing his spacious bungalow at Osborne. He was always at hand to accept graciously any
gifts the Queen had to bestow. He remained in enjoyment of an
ample salary and his office was still open. It was concerned with
what might be called the social and ceremonial problems involved in
the governing of India, so whatever the truth about his background
he could no longer be of significance in the revolutionary councils
of that country. He continued to hold daily conversations in
Hindustani with the Queen and to appear to many as an all too
familiar figure near her person.

'Jackie' Fisher, writing after one of his spells as the Queen's guest
at Osborne in the late nineties, speaks of the Munshi as a Court
irritant, who was still so favoured by the Queen that the outraged
feelings of ladies and gentlemen boiled up from time to time to the
verge of mutiny and resignation.

PART SIX

'Granny-Gran' the Glorious

13

'Granny-Gran' at Home and Abroad

THE span of the nineties, the *fin de siècle*, may well be called the era of 'GRANNY-GRAN' the GLORIOUS. Perhaps Queen Victoria, lame, old and slowly losing her sight, was truly more happy and more herself as she basked in this golden sunshine of her age-worn Queenhood than ever before. She was the great royal Granny-Gran not only to Britons but to the wondering nations of the Continent. The flashing young Tsar of All the Russias called her 'Granny' in a tone of reverential devotion though not one drop of her blood ran in his veins. Kaiser William of Germany, the bristling bully of Europe hailed her as 'the most unparalleled Grandmama as ever existed'. Frenchmen uncovered in breathless awe before the splendour of her majesty while cursing and scorning the vile perfidious British.

In 1892 when Kaiser William was being exceptionally rash and difficult, the Queen, then staying at Hyères, received a suggestion from Lord Salisbury that it might prove very useful if, when she went on to Darmstadt, she would seek a personal interview with him in order to quieten him down. This annoyed her and she scribbled an answer to the Private Secretary, which he scarcely felt he could relay to Lord Salisbury.

'—No, no, I really cannot go about keeping everybody in order!'

But it so happened that William also had an idea that it would be advantageous to see his grandmother. He therefore asked Princess Marie Louise, who had become the wife of Prince Aubert of Anhalt and who was regarded as the Queen's agent in Germany, to write and tell the Queen that he greatly desired her to visit him in Berlin. A long letter reached Marie Louise a few days later. It described in great detail her holiday in Italy. But there was a postscript:

'Tell William that I appreciate his wish to see me. However, in my opinion it would be more fitting if the grandson were to travel to see his aged grandmother than that she should undertake a long and tiring journey to see him.'

The Kaiser set out for Darmstadt and respectfully presented himself before his Granny.

An interesting occasion at Osborne happened in this year when that man who emphatically did not admire the Queen came to dine with her. It was the day when Mr Gladstone entered upon his last Prime Ministership with the firm resolve to give the Irish Home Rule in defiance of the Queen's determination to withhold it from them. The veteran statesman, feeble and bending from his great height, with the lean neck and wasted countenance of a museum mummy but with eyes restless and blazing, had journeyed triumphantly to the Isle of Wight to see the Queen.

That night Henry Ponsonby and his newly married daughter Alberta were among the guests at the Queen's table, and Alberta, entirely fresh to the ways in the royal homes, has left a striking record of the event.

The guests were all gathered in the drawing-room when at 8.30 the Queen 'swept in'. Those words of Alberta's are surely an impressive tribute to the Queen's majesty: for what the young woman actually saw was an aged lady hobbling with a stick and leaning heavily on the arm of an Indian servant. Mr Gladstone, too, had his supporting stick.

It was perfectly plain to Alberta as the Queen surveyed the drawing-room that she was aware only of the presence of one person – Mr Gladstone; that she intensely disliked him and that Gladstone in his turn fully understood the reason for the malevolence shining in the royal eyes. The old man was 'nervously fumbling over his stick'.

The Queen unhesitantly advanced upon him, took his hand and with a hyena-like smile proclaimed, 'You and I, Mr Gladstone, are much lamer than we used to be!'

The Prime Minister muttered and bowed jerkily with a confused air. Then, as if it were an afterthought, he snatched at the Queen's hand and abruptly kissed it. The Queen examined him coldly:

'This should have been done this afternoon,' she announced.

He had seen her for a few minutes when he first arrived, but had forgotten in his embarrassment to perform this ritual ceremony for a new Prime Minister.

The Queen then turned her back and made for the dining-room at a surprising speed. Alberta had always been told that royal dinner parties were conducted in an awed whisper, unless the Queen was in exceptional spirits, which certainly did not appear to be the case that night. Seated next to Mr Gladstone, she was surprised therefore when he presently started to address her in a loud and eager voice. He was indignant about something; but she was so frightened by the attention drawn to her that she did not know what he was saying. Looking up she saw the Queen's 'piercing eye' upon them, but *H.M.* kept her silence. Alberta's discomfort grew, but in a kind of nightmare she heard Gladstone expounding to her the inestimable benefits of Irish Home Rule, a subject concerning which she had learnt from her father the vehemence of the Queen's opinions. In misery and shame she studied the tablecloth while Gladstone rolled out his phrases.

Perhaps the Queen's hearing was not so keen as it had been in the old days, and she was only aware that Mr Gladstone was making an unseemly noise. 'After dinner the Queen came straight up to me,' records Alberta, 'and asked, "What did Mr Gladstone talk to you about?" – "Home Rule, ma'am!" She shrugged her shoulders and said, "I know! – he always will!".'

When Frederick Ponsonby had arrived at Osborne from India to take up his duties as Extra-Equerry, the reluctant young guardsman was going from a life of gaiety and bustle, colour and ceremonial in the glittering Viceregal orbit to a strange, creeping existence of ghostly half-shadows and chilling restrictions. He was lucky to possess his father's sense of humour.

The régime prevailing inside the house at Osborne was a field of discovery for him. It was by then a home of old people, who were set in their ways. Only among the Ladies were the comparatively young sometimes to be met with in the course of their Waiting. The perpetual silence in the great house was unnerving. Whatever this place might have seemed like to mid-Victorians under the spell of the Great Exhibition it seemed terrible to his generation, as indeed it did to some who were considerably older. He was told that Lord Rosebery was in the habit of declaring that the Osborne drawing-room was the ugliest, most uncomfortable room in the world, and gazing at its pointless arcades of horribly pseudo classical pillars, its forest-like clutter and jumbled masses of colours, he understood its depressive qualities.

When the Queen went out in the afternoons she only required an equerry when driving through Cowes, Newport or Ryde, so that frequently there was no call on them after luncheon. The Queen being gone it had become the custom for all members of the household to slip out for a walk, and it was equally traditional that all must take different paths and promenade alone. This may have developed out of a kind of blind urge for protective dispersion on these clandestine expeditions, and Frederick Ponsonby describes the unsociable scene of departure when all darted anxiously into the open and fanned out round the house as 'like a lunatic asylum'.

Frederick soon had personal experience of the Queen's detestation of smoking. Having little to do he was often employed in deciphering telegrams in the Equerries' room. A note was brought to him by the Queen saying he must *never* smoke when doing this, as when she had received the box holding his decoded telegrams she had been disgusted by a strong odour of tobacco.

The Queen had fallen into a way of leaving it until very late before she stated whom of the household she wished to dine with her that night. The method of invitation used was for a footman to poke his head round the door of the Ladies-in-Waiting drawing-room and the Equerries' room and grunt brusquely, 'All 'ere dines with the Queen!' – or selecting victims like a sergeant-major he would snap, 'You – you and you for the Queen's Dinner!'

Frederick's first Osborne misfortune took place at night. The hall at Osborne was lined with statues and these were reputed to revolve on their pedestals. It was quite late when he happened to pass through the hall with Colonel Harry Legge, and felt suddenly impelled to exhibit the unusual quality of the statues to his companion. He was working entirely on hearsay and had never touched one before. The statue he selected at once toppled off the pedestal on top of him.

He and Legge strained every muscle to thrust the figure back into place. Sagging under the weight they collapsed with it to the floor. With horror Frederick pocketed a chip which had come off the face and thought of the eagle eye of the Queen. But the most urgent need was to return the statue to the pedestal that night while the hall was deserted. They found two footmen and brought them to the hall. Even this muscular quartette were unable to lift the detestable statue from the ground. The others declared their intention of abandoning it for the night, and the culprit crept away to a sleepless bed.

Early in the morning the frightened new Equerry was out in the grounds looking for estate workmen. He found some and led them into the hall. There he regarded them hopefully while they regarded him and the statue without enthusiasm. At first he was afraid they meant to leave him to face his fate with the prostrate statue, but they went off and returned with a block and tackle. The stillness of the sleeping house was broken by the noise of creaking, the shouting of morose orders and the clatter of nailed boots on the marble. The workmen retired having returned the statue to its place.

The Queen always heard about everything and was certain to ask questions, even if she did not find the chip off the statue. Frederick confessed to Princess Beatrice, who told him it would be wisest for her to tell the Queen. The result of this was a note in the Queen's handwriting, which next day circulated among members of the household: '*Nobody must touch the statues, and certainly not play with them.*' Most of the old men, not having heard of the misadventure, were much perplexed and mildly insulted, and the Ladies being curious by nature set to work to find the explanation.

The young Equerry accompanied the Queen to Balmoral and

there made his second mistake. The King of Portugal was coming to stay with the Queen, and Frederick was told to arrange with the housekeeper that suitable rooms should be provided for all the Portuguese suite. As usual the Castle was already lodging many more people than was necessary, and the housekeeper protested that she simply could not provide a bedroom for one of the Portuguese. When she suggested that a Maid of Honour then expected to come into Waiting might be deferred for a week, Ponsonby assured her it was an excellent idea and he would write to the Queen.

His letter went up in the box and later in the day returned with the Queen's blue-pencilled comment underneath it.

'—The Queen has yet to learn that Captain Ponsonby has anything to do with the Maids of Honour.'

Upon opening his note the Queen had known exactly what must be done to house the superfluous Portuguese.

'Nonsense,' she had snapped to Lady Ampthill, 'We must double up!'

In the gloom of Balmoral the Ghillies' Balls, as frequent as ever, came as a shock to Frederick Ponsonby. He was used to guest-night frolics in the mess; but in such a setting these Highland dances appeared positively bacchanalian. The Queen could no longer dance the Hoolichan, but he observed with wonder her childish appreciation at the rising tempo of the scene before her, and her eagerness to offer her younger female guests to the tender care of tipsy ghillies, who mopping their brows came plunging up to the royal dais.

After a year of service had passed for Frederick Ponsonby the Queen had still not spoken to him since their original interview. But in 1895 he accompanied her to the South of France. Cimiez, near Nice, had become her favourite place for holidays. He felt that on this occasion she must surely break her silence, for the only Gentlemen to go with her apart from himself were Sir Arthur Bigge, Sir Fleetwood Edwards, Sir James Reid and Colonel Davidson, Groom-in-Waiting. But it did not happen throughout all those long tedious days they spent in near imprisonment at the Hotel Excelsior, although he was sometimes employed within a few feet of her.

The Queen went for her last drive before her departure for England, and by virtue of his office Frederick rode beside the carriage in top hat and frockcoat with strapped trousers. When on their return the carriage stopped before the Excelsior he quickly dismounted and took up his position on guard to ward off intruders at the reverse door of the carriage to that from which the Queen descended. As the Queen rose she looked at him and exclaimed: 'What a pity it is to leave Nice in such beautiful weather.'

She had turned her back and was hobbling into the Excelsior. It had happened at last and he was so stunned he had not even nodded intelligently. It was not much; but it was a beginning. Several months were to pass before she noticed him again. Nevertheless, those words inaugurated the first real step forward in a brilliant career.

In the nineties the Queen's holidays abroad, which had previously been pursued with more or less casual informality in company with but a humble train of attendants, attained to the heroic proportions of an Odyssean adventure. In the old days even servants selected for the royal continental travels had allowed themselves a freedom of speech and manner, which though believed to be agreeable to *H.M.* on foreign soil, they would never have attempted at home. Now each was but one of a stern band of praetorians dedicated to preserve the grandeur of the old White Goddess.

The Queen used to travel from Folkestone using the R.Y. *Victoria*, landing at Cherbourg or Boulogne. Although the personal suite was small she now took with her so many attendants that her party numbered one hundred or more. At Folkestone she always ordered the covered gangway to be put down so that the huge crowds could not watch her being carried aboard in her chair by sailors. The police rigidly enforced her instructions to keep the spectators at a considerable distance.

Although she still travelled unofficially, she had dropped all pretence of being the Countess of Balmoral, and strongly as she complained of the fuss which greeted her directly she reached French soil, her wrath would have been terrible had any Frenchman

attempted to treat her as a mere holidaying Countess. As her chair
emerged from the covered gangway at Cherbourg or Boulogne
she would see before her a red velvet tent trimmed with gold lace.
She would rise and the Mayor and his dignitaries would conduct her
slowly across the quay to a gilded chair waiting in the tent, while a
red-legged Guard of Honour presented arms, the massed bands and
bugles of the garrison blared and the crowds roared and struggled
with Gallic abandon. When Her Majesty had been seated in the
gilded chair the local Generals, Admirals, Senators and officials
formed a rank and waited expectantly to be summoned for a greeting
by the Presence. They were sometimes disappointed when the
Queen was contented with the honours offered by the Mayor.
Throughout the whole of the nineties Britons were unpopular in
France; but the jubilant welcome to the Queen did not abate, even
in the latter years when British tourists might be stoned, chased or
spat upon.

Up till 1895 the Queen lived at the Hotel Excelsior at Cimiez and
she took over the whole building for the period of her stay. Although
she had comparatively few guests to stay with her the inhabitants of
the building always went about with the feeling that the walls were
about to split asunder and all but the most exalted endured the
Queen's holiday in barrack-like discomfort. Masters of the Household had several times gone to the Queen before the departure after
being presented with the staggering list of servants marked down 'to
travel'. The Queen after politely perusing the list would shake her
head and declare, 'No – I've checked every name. I can't spare one
of them!'

The French always put a military guard on the Hotel Excelsior, and
two delighted French officers used to come into residence. They were
the only members of the household who enjoyed the royal holiday.
Palace life was a grand adventure to them and their loyalty to the
Queen Empress far outdid that of her own attendants. But for all
their exertions these energetic warriors were unable to stop the
sightseers from bursting into the grounds of the Excelsior to watch
the Queen sitting at her table under an awning with an Indian

beside her. It was largely on the score of these unpredictable invasions that the Queen began to think the Excelsior an unsatisfactory residence, and when in 1895 she was offered the more secluded and more spacious *Villa Liserbe* for future holidays, she informed the management that she would not be coming again.

One of the sad events in 1895 was the death from fever of Prince Henry of Battenberg, who had volunteered for the Ashanti campaign. Some said he did this out of sheer desperation. Protests would not stop him. He saw no action, for the fever quickly seized upon him and he died at sea on the way home.

The Queen was deeply upset by the loss of the son-in-law who had served her so well, although some thought that she was secretly glad that Beatrice would now be free to devote herself wholly to her for the rest of her life.

Princess Marie Louise tells of an event following the death of Prince Henry in which Lady Errol, one of those fatuous faithful women whom the Queen delighted to love and bully, earned herself one of the celebrated royal snubs.

Following the tragedy the Queen was left in a mood of the deepest gloom at Osborne, and Lady Errol (Leila), who had suffered a good deal in consequence, thought it was time to bring the Queen out of her depression. The first step was always a hazard with the Queen, and Leila decided that some elevating and soothing remark which would encourage her to talk about her grief was the right thing.

'Oh, Your Majesty,' she sighed, 'think when we all shall meet our dear ones once again in Heaven!'

'Yes,' muttered the Queen. Silence lasting about a minute followed. Leila tried again.

'We will all meet in Abraham's bosom,' she ventured in sepulchral tones.

Silence for half a minute.

'—I will NOT meet Abraham!' hissed the Queen.

Leila had always been insufferably silly on occasions, and that night the Queen called up her lingering displeasure in her journal. *'Dear Leila, not at all consoling in moments of trouble!'*

Reggie Brett (Lord Esher), who in this year took over the Secretary-ship of the Office of Works, has recorded a picture of the Queen in one of her considerate moods: Lord Rosebery was the subject of her kindness, and it was he who told Brett about his experience.

When he took over the Prime Ministership he was recovering from a severe attack of influenza, and acute insomnia and sudden bouts of giddiness were the after-effects. When he reached Windsor to present himself to the Queen people assured him that he looked terrible and he certainly felt it. He was dreading the meeting with the Queen, for he well knew what a wearing experience this could be even to the most robust, and he was hoping he could succeed in keeping on his feet during a long interview. He was aware that no Minister but Disraeli had ever sat in the Queen's presence – and that was a joke. He did not flatter himself that *H.M.* had any soft feeling for him which might prompt her to give him a like invitation.

As soon as the Queen saw him she caught his hand and told him to sit down. He protested. She commanded him to take a chair.

At the close of the interview it was necessary for him to kneel and kiss the Queen's hand. Such an exercise requires balance and he knew he had little. He dropped on one knee with his head swimming and as he struggled to keep himself from toppling over he heard the Queen cry out, 'Take care!' and felt her hands steady him just enough to enable him to right his equilibrium.

By 1896 Frederick Ponsonby's position at Court was improving. He could not help feeling that the Queen was casting a friendly, almost a motherly, eye on her youngest Equerry. For himself, he as yet scarcely regarded his duties as earnestly as he might have done and was not sure that the military life was not preferable. Frederick, therefore, did not shrink from risking the royal wrath from time to time.

The Queen objected to her Gentlemen dining out when in Waiting, and should any have the temerity to ask to do so she generally found some reason why she wished him to dine at her table that night. As a rule, those who were to attend Queen's

Dinner at Windsor were warned of this early in the day; but the Queen had been known to alter plans at the last moment.

One night in this year Frederick Ponsonby decided to take a chance. He accepted an invitation to dine at the Guards barracks at 7.30 p.m. and join a theatre party afterwards. Unhappily for him, when leaving the Castle gates in evening dress he passed the Queen's piper coming in. He had recently fallen foul of this important personage because he had caught him after a big Queen's Dinner treating the Scots Guards band to the wine and dessert left on the table.

The Queen's piper, as was later discovered, told one of the Queen's dressers to tell Her Majesty that the Junior Equerry had gone out of the Castle. Immediately the Queen ordered the Master of the Household to put Captain Ponsonby's name on her 9 p.m. Dinner list. Ponsonby's servant was told by a footman at 8.15 that his master was 'dining with the Queen'. He was a man of resource. He sprinted out of the Castle past an astonished sentry, who watched him with extreme suspicion, caught a cab and at full gallop came pounding into the barrack square.

Frederick had reached that stage of the dinner when he was in towering spirits; but he was not so gay that he could not instantly realize the horror of his situation. Abandoning cigar and coffee he fled from the table and plunged into the waiting cab.

The homeward journey was frantic; but more laboured. The old horse was blown. The hill was long and steep. The cabby shouted at the horse and Frederick shouted at the cabby. Queen's Dinners were never late, and there were but a few minutes in hand when Frederick dived from the cab and panted up to his room.

But when the Queen came to lead her party in to dinner her eyes lighted upon the Junior Equerry, who in Windsor coat, breeches and buckled shoes, bowed to her with happy equanimity.

At the table Frederick ploughed courageously through every course, watched intently by the Queen, and not being entirely sobered by the shock of his escape felt impelled in defiance of warning glances from his seniors to do his garrulous best to enliven a more than usually awed and tongue-tied party of guests.

There was one terrible night when the Senior Equerry, a very ancient warrior, forgot to warn the Lifeguards stationed at Windsor that their band was wanted for a big Queen's Dinner. The poor old man discovered his mistake almost at the last moment. He was nearly suicidal and tears were in his eyes when Frederick Ponsonby came upon him. Never in the Queen's long reign had a military band failed to appear when she required it. After so many years of loyal service he would die discharged and disgraced by his Sovereign. Nothing could be done now.

Frederick realized that if he sent a galloper to the Lifeguards it might still be possible to bring their band to the Castle in time, even if the bandsmen had to be snatched out of the public houses of the town. At least it was worth making the attempt.

But one baffling problem had to be overcome. At Queen's Dinners the band played on the little terrace outside the tall dining-room windows, and the only way to reach this terrace, which was high above the ground, was through the dining-room. Thus, while a noisy and indignant band was stumbling with clashing instruments through the dining-room, the Queen with her Indian servant and her dinner-guests might march in on their heels, and if she did so her fury would know no bounds. It would be almost worse for the Senior Equerry than if there were no band at all. What was to be done?

Frederick thought of ladders. Directly the galloper had been ordered out he hurried to the house of the Surveyor of Works, who was fortunately at home. The problem was explained. At first the shocked Surveyor was reluctant to engage himself in such a trans-action, fearful for himself if the Queen discovered that he had joined in a plot to fool her. But Frederick was persuasive. When he left he had obtained a promise that ladders would be placed so that the band could scale the parapet of the terrace from the outside.

The rest had to be left to chance. Frederick Ponsonby had to be with the Queen at the dinner and could not stand below to urge the reluctant and bewildered bandsmen to mount the ladders with their instruments, which in some cases must be heavy and clumsy. There might be accidents. There was likely to be no little commotion in the evening quiet of the Castle as the assault on the terrace took place, causing people to gaze down from windows. The bandmaster, a most exclusive person, might protest at such an indignity, or even refuse to lend himself to such an irregular operation.

The hour of Dinner arrived. The Queen at the head of her important guests moved majestically into the dining-room. No National Anthem greeted her. In surprise she peered towards the open terrace windows. The night which they framed showed blank darkness, and in silence the Queen with a puzzled air enthroned herself with her back to the windows. In an agony the Senior Equerry sat shaking and composing his resignation.

Frederick, entering last, gazed unhappily towards the open windows. The Queen, having important guests to deal with, immediately opened a conversation, and at this moment Frederick saw human forms struggling on to the parapet against the night sky. The stealth and speed of the soldiers on the terrace was a triumph of military discipline. Suddenly with a kind of frenzied gasp the strains of a popular musical comedy burst out, so urgent at first that it drowned the talkers but quickly modulated to a seemly pitch by the bandmaster.

The sound of the music appeared to please the Queen, who did not seem to be unduly surprised or put out by its lateness in starting. But next morning she complained against the bandmaster of the Lifeguards for failing to play the National Anthem. Her displeasure was expressed to the Senior Equerry, who was supposed to convey it to the Lifeguards. Frederick Ponsonby never knew how his senior contrived to excuse the bandmaster for the shaken old gentleman preferred never afterwards to mention the most fearful incident of his life; but always understood he had contrived to do so by raking up some antiquated custom which satisfied the Queen. Although she was supposed to get to hear about everything which went wrong the secret drama of that night was a story which never penetrated to her.

It was during this period that Cecil Rhodes, on leave from South Africa, was summoned to dine with the Queen. Rhodes was then at the apex of his glory, the greatest of the Empire builders, and the Queen's attitude towards him which was unwittingly revealed by herself to the Duchess of Buccleugh shortly after this event is a striking example of how the presence of *men of action* worked upon her. She was used to inspiring terror in people much cleverer and abler than herself and could baffle their calculated overtures with crushing shrewdness; but the heroic giants – Rhodes, Lord Cromer, Garnet-Wolseley and later Kitchener, overwhelmed her. She listened to them with girlish naïvety, she struggled to reach their Olympian heights and when they left her she was breathless with awe.

The Duchess of Buccleugh, like many notable hostesses, had avoided Cecil Rhodes when he was in London as she believed that he despised women and treated them with insulting brevity. Having listened to the Queen's glowing description of the great pioneer when at Windsor she told her that she had never met him and did not intend to do so, as she objected to the prospect of being rebuffed by him. The Queen regarded her with a puzzled expression.

'Oh, I don't think that can be so,' she declared. 'He was very civil to me when he came down to Windsor!'

14

'Granny-Gran' roaring to the End

THERE is a photograph taken by Charles Knight in 1898 of the Queen as she sat in her carriage on some public occasion. It is a unique photograph; for it is the only existing one which shows the Queen smiling broadly – or, indeed, smiling at all. True, in this photograph, where she looks much younger than in all the solemn ones of the time, she might be mistaken for *Charley's Aunt* or any old flower seller sitting on the steps of Eros in Piccadilly Circus; but none can doubt that the chubby, smooth-cheeked matron with shining eyes whom the camera had caught is a happy woman at peace with herself.

For such an old lady, the Queen, although fretful and tyrannical in little things, was possessed of astonishing coolness and serenity in calamity, as is proved by the adventure of the brown roans. This might well have ended most dismally and badly shocked a much younger person.

The Queen had been persuaded to adopt a pair of roan horses for her private drives in place of the greys which she had always favoured in the past. The roans gave some trouble and the old coachman, who did not like them, was not the only one to suggest that the Queen would be wise to give them up. She ignored the advice.

One afternoon at Windsor, Marie Louise was summoned from her room. It was an urgent message by the Queen. She ran out and almost tumbled headfirst over her grandmother, who lay across a small passage off the corridor. Out of a bundle of black garments – 'half-sitting, half-lying' – the pale and moon-like face of the Queen shone in the gloom, and peering up owlishly she gasped out a story of woe.

The roans had bolted and the carriage had turned over.

'—a terrible accident, my dear!'

The voice had grown clearer as the narrative proceeded and the teller seemed to be deriving increasing pleasure from it. At the end the big scared eyes twinkled.

'Dear Frankie Clark (Highland footman) lifted me out of the carriage,' she announced, '—and, would you believe it – all my petticoats came undone!'

1897 was a significant year in the life of Frederick Ponsonby. The post of Assistant Private Secretary had fallen vacant and the Queen announced that she would be pleased for him to take the post.

He knew that it was a 'command', and people were considered unwise if they did not fall in with her plans. But it would mean his resignation from the Grenadier Guards, and had he not felt so strongly that his father would have wanted him to accept he would have been tempted to refuse the Queen however dire might be the result. He accepted; but it was not without mental reservations. There were some aspects of life with the Queen which he regarded in a spirit of indignation or derision, and as yet he was not ready to give himself wholeheartedly to her. His father had always been a cynic in his service; but an utterly devoted, gentle cynic. Frederick up to that time had experienced very little personal contact with the Queen in spite of being so close to her so often, and, in fact, he would not at first do so in his new office.

Although he knew he must be in the Queen's good books – she had taken to calling him 'Fritz', though sometimes with a stern and penetrating look – he was somewhat at a loss to know why, and he was in 1897 still careless of that honour. He was still making *gaffes*, and was moved rather to laugh over them than to feel ashamed and terrified as an earnest courtier should have done.

There had been an evening at Balmoral during a family dinner party, which Frederick had attended, when he had unintentionally pronounced a severe stricture on the intelligence of the Queen, which was heard by everybody.

The Empress Frederick of Germany was staying with her mother.

She started a conversation on books. It was not a subject upon which the Queen was really at home, since only the most popular brands of literature had any appeal at all; but she desired to keep her end up with her intellectual daughter.

'—I suppose,' remarked the Queen, 'that Marie Corelli will be hailed by posterity as about the finest author of this age.'

The Empress was stunned, and everybody who had heard this royal pronouncement was surprised and amused.

'Mother! – you can't believe that,' cried the Empress. 'All her novels are trash!'

The Empress gazed round the table with a look of appeal, and her eyes caught those of Frederick Ponsonby. He had been dreaming and had not heard a word of the conversation.

'Fritz,' said the Empress, 'what do you think of Marie Corelli's books?'

He thought her novels quite good, but knowing how clever the Empress was he thought he should make some announcement which would impress her. He paused in order to give weight to his opinion.

'—Well,' he declared, 'I think the secret of the huge sales of her novels is simply that she appeals to the semi-educated.'

He was startled when the Empress clapped her hands and laughed in her mother's face, and had no idea until later why silence had suddenly descended on the table.

Yet 'Fritz' could boast of a privilege accorded to him by the Queen at that time, which was unique to the point of being historical.

The Queen's favourite place abroad was still Cimiez, although Anglo-French relations had grown so explosive and reports of ill-used English tourists so common, that even she used to debate whether she dared to risk going to France. But she always went, and the French always greeted her as if she was Queen of France.

Life at the *Villa Liserbe* was more peaceful for her than it had been at the Excelsior. She had grown more liberal to her Gentlemen, if not to her Ladies, and if they were not wanted in the afternoons they

might take the train to Monte Carlo to amuse themselves at the
Casino. It appeared to give her much delight to enter men in her
Dinner List whom she knew had gone to Monte Carlo. She would
then alter the List at about six o'clock, but that did not matter if
they caught the right train home. Frederick Ponsonby was forced to
embark on many a race between the Casino and Monte Carlo
station. Astonishingly enough, his luck always held, although once
his career hung dangerously in the balance when, upon leaping
desperately into a carriage on the moving train, he was confronted
by a frantic lady convinced that his aim was to assault her. The train
was stopped; but he fortunately managed to convince everybody of
the truth.

One of the weekly features of *Villa Liserbe* was the Sunday
service held on the premises. For this the household, both the upper
and the lower strata, combined to form a scratch choir. A great deal
of practise had to be undergone by the members as the Queen took
almost as much interest in their performances as in her private
theatricals. When anything went wrong she was deeply annoyed and
wished to know the reason why. Her questions were always directed
at 'Fritz', whom she regarded as the choir's leader.

One of the most sensational events at *Villa Liserbe* happened in
April 1898 when the Queen received Felix Faure, the President of
the French Republic. As head of a great State, Faure was entitled to
be received with all the honours due to a Sovereign; but the Queen
was unwilling to accept this point of view. The fact that the Prince
of Wales, who was at Cimiez and whom she still sometimes publicly
scolded like an ill-conducted schoolboy, was strongly urging her to
observe every formal courtesy to the President only strengthened
her resolve to regard him as a kind of upstart inferior.

'I would not go down to the front door to welcome the President,'
she declared, 'even if I were a younger woman. He can come upstairs
to meet me.'

The Prince of Wales, growing indignant, told her that whatever
she chose to do, he, of course, would be at the door to receive the
Head of the French State.

'Do nothing of the kind!' ordered the Queen. 'It will be quite good enough if you meet him at the top of the stairs.'

The Prince knew very well that this would *not* be good enough, but he dared not go down to the hall in defiance of his mother. He decided to make the best of a bad business by pretending to be late. His intention was to lurk on the first floor out of sight of the stair-head. As the President stepped through the front door he would charge breathlessly to the top of the stairs and rush down to greet him effusively and apologetically half-way.

The day and the hour arrived, and President Faure strode into the hall of *Villa Liserbe*. Only small fry were gathered to meet him – Arthur Bigge, Frederick Ponsonby and Ladies-in-Waiting. The President subjected them to a hard scrutiny and dismissed them. Then his glance ranged expectantly round the hall. He had broken a journey especially to call upon the Queen, and as a Frenchman expected his money's worth. To further emphasize the rising indignation expressed in his looks he kept his top hat on his head.

Still hatted the President marched towards the stairs and began to stump glumly upwards. Suddenly the Prince of Wales jumped dramatically to the stairhead, executed a mime of astonishment, and bounded down muttering apologies. A collision was averted. The President's face had brightened at once. The performance appeared to have been successful, and he was able to remove his hat.

In the presence of the Queen, President Faure behaved with all the aplomb of a cultured Frenchman. But he wished her to realize that he was for all practical purposes a fellow Sovereign, and he subtly directed the conversation in such a way that she could not avoid understanding him. They were neither of them assisting the improvement of Anglo-French relations. After a quarter of an hour, the Queen rose, supported on her stick, and bade him farewell, informing him dryly that France was a beautiful country. He awarded the Queen a cool but sufficiently low bow, and then as a fellow Sovereign turned his back and walked from the room. The Queen was exceedingly angry.

Naturally reports of the President's shabby treatment at the *Villa Liserbe* reached Paris, and the French were more than ready to be seized with fearful wrath – until they heard with horror of the grossly ill-bred behaviour of their President in the Queen's hall. For a few days, at least, our tourists were treated with rather more consideration by the French.

On 19 May, Gladstone died. He had had many enemies, but nearly everybody thought he should have a State funeral. It was an occasion for the Queen to display the least noble side of her character. She declared that he had no right to one because he was not a Minister in office at the time of his death. It was true: she was fully entitled not to grant him this honour. But she shocked those who heard her, and they let her see it. In the end she gave her permission, but it was in a manner of suppressed scorn.

She was filled with anger when she heard that the Prince of Wales had offered to be one of the pall-bearers at the State funeral, and that his offer had been accepted by Mrs Gladstone. She had been warned too late and dared not forbid her son to honour his offer, because of the scandal this would cause. She was even more outraged and openly expressed her indignation upon being told that the Prince of Wales had kissed the hand of Mrs Gladstone after the funeral.

It had been earnestly suggested to the Queen that she should personally write an appreciation of Gladstone's great services to the nation, and that this should be circulated to the Press. She absolutely refused:

'I am sorry for Mrs Gladstone,' she declared '—as for him – I never liked him and I will say nothing about him!'

The work of organizing the State funeral fell largely upon Reginald Brett, and as he was used to being often in communication with the Queen over the work of his Department, he expected to receive some instructions from her about it. He heard nothing; nor did he receive any answer to letters he had sent in on the subject. When in June he went to dine with her at Windsor he was, in his own words, 'gently rebuked for misdirected enthusiasm over the Ceremonial last month'.

May was also the month when the Queen visited Netley Military Hospital. She was wheeled round the wards in her chair. Two celebrated Sudan V.C's, Piper Findlater and Private Vickery, were waiting seated in one of the wards and the Queen was to present them with their decorations. As the Queen approached the two wounded men the Commandant signalled to them to stand. The Queen saw them labouring to do so.

'Most certainly not!' she cried out indignantly. She raised herself in her chair before it had stopped moving, stepped down and, almost before anybody realized what was happening, was bending over the men and pinning on the Crosses. This was said to be the first time she had moved unaided for several years.

This was also the first time the Queen was seen in public wearing spectacles. This had become very necessary; but she did not like them for she thought – rightly – that they made her look very 'common'. The result, as she expected, was that the press artists supplied the illustrated journals with most unattractive sketches of her in her spectacles.

During this year the Queen was growing increasingly blind, but she contrived to keep most people unaware of this. 'Fritz' Ponsonby, however, had good cause to know the truth. She had come to rely on him a great deal, and he was used to her calling out, 'Fritz – do this' – 'Fritz – do that', when she believed he was in the room but could not distinguish him. At first these often petulant demands irritated him until it dawned on him that she was appealing to an unseen friend.

The Queen's handwriting began to become contorted and almost illegible: a very serious matter in view of her persistence in doing business by notes, and her new Assistant Private Secretary spent much of his time puzzling over these and making fair copies before distributing them to those for whom they were intended. He was startled to find himself writing such phrases as *Bertie and Alix must not do this* – '*William (the Kaiser) is quite wrong, he should remember, etc., etc.*' and he had to put in the strong underlinings whenever she did so. He also began to receive notes of complaint from the Queen saying that his own letters sent up to her were so carelessly written that they were wholly unreadable.

Sometimes the Queen glossed over mistakes caused by her blindness with great skill. There was an odd tradition at Windsor that the Lord-in-Waiting arranged the seating at the Queen's Dinners, and sometimes he put the wrong people together with most unhappy results. He was supposed to observe one unwritten law: he must seat the most important guest on the right of the Queen. This could lead to mistakes, for it was not always easy to decide whom the Queen would consider her most important guest and the Lord-in-Waiting sometimes suffered agonies of anxiety over his choice. One night the French Ambassador and the Italian Ambassador were to dine with the Queen. The seating problem in this case was simple: M. Cambon of France being the senior, sat on Her Majesty's right and the Italian Ambassador on her left; but Lord Harris somehow mixed the seat cards. When the party took their seats the Ambassadors were reversed, and the Queen, unable to distinguish their faces, did not know this.

It was her invariable custom to converse first with her least important neighbour, and then to turn and pursue a much longer conversation with the right-hand guest. Accordingly, she turned left and believing the Italian Ambassador to be on that side addressed M. Cambon of France.

'Where is your King now?' she inquired.

Cambon, the veteran republican diplomat, although nobody had warned him that the Queen was blind, did not turn a hair. By luck his morning newspaper had told him something of the movement of the King of Italy.

'I believe, Ma'am, the King is cruising in his yacht,' he answered with composure.

The Queen recognized the French accent, and knew what had happened.

She, too, was a veteran. Not one flicker of an eyelid betrayed her. Inwardly she was raging against Lord Harris. In sepulchral tones she carried straight on with a conversation acceptable equally to a

Frenchman or an Italian, and then switched over and engaged the
Italian in the same non-committal brand of talk. Nobody was
embarrassed, and neither Ambassador was sure at the time that the
Queen had perceived her mistake.

But she sent for Lord Harris as soon as they had taken their leave,
and after a stormy interview he crept away utterly crushed to his
bedroom.

Fritz Ponsonby during his few years of service with the Queen
had, from the time she decided that she liked him and began to
single him out, suffered from worries in his personal life. He was one
of those victims of that terrifying passion of possessiveness which
from time to time surged up in the Queen. He had wanted to marry
in 1896. The Queen would not hear of this. It was his father's story
over again.

'He will tell my private affairs to his wife,' she declared, 'and
everything will go the round of London!'

From that time on he had been secretly restless, and doubtless the
woman of his choice was not inclined to be for ever patient with him
for falling in with the Queen's whims. Was he to be a bachelor as
long as he lived?

When 1899 came he had endured long enough. To foil him the
Queen began to find excuses for not seeing him, or if she did, only
when he could not possibly use the occasion to plead his cause. The
Honourable Miss Phipps, the Senior Woman of the Bedchamber,
took up his cause for him and argued daily with the Queen until she
at last gave her consent to his marriage. But she stipulated that Fritz
was to be warned that she would *never* give him a house!

He was married in that year. All the royal daughters pleaded with
their mother to allot a house to Fritz. There were suitable vacancies.
Only her consent was needed. The Empress Frederick, ever confident, practically promised Fritz that she would get him one. They
all failed.

When in the Autumn of 1899 the Boer War broke out it so
happened that Sir Arthur Bigge had to be absent from Court for
some time, and Fritz Ponsonby was called upon to be Acting-Private

Secretary. Up to that time he had never been alone with the Queen.

Now he was summoned to the Closet at all hours, and learned to abandon his papers with patience in order to deal with the most trivial matters. For the first time he truly realized what his father must have borne in the days when the Queen was younger and more aggressively difficult. His new experience was not altogether unenjoyable. The Queen fascinated him as she had Sir Henry.

There were moments when something caused the aged Queen to be so rocked by laughter that he hovered over her, 'afraid she would have a fit'.

One morning he brought her a memorandum, which sought her consent for the Royal Irish Fusiliers to wear a green plume in their busbies. The memorandum was written very large, but momentarily her powerful reading-glasses betrayed her. The Queen read *'breeches'* instead of *'busbies'*. Then the absurdity of that struck her:

'Fritz', she exclaimed, 'I wonder where would be the best place for the Royal Irish to wear a green hackle on their breeches!'

But more often in those war days – the shock and humiliation of the *Black Week* had come and gone – Fritz watched her 'break down and cry at the long list of casualties'. The scent of battle had revitalized her, and even when the martial hysteria of the nation quailed she faced disaster with a balanced mind which put to shame many of her subjects, high and low.

The great defeats caused the leading clergy, with truly Victorian piety, to propose a day of National Humiliation.

'I don't like the idea,' snapped the Queen. 'Let them pray. I hope they will do so, but it should be without order from me. Why humiliate ourselves if right. If the war is wrong – the sooner they stop it the better.'

The public who had cheered the soldiers off to war with so much clamorous excitement, the journalists who had scribbled so much heroic nonsense about them, the high officials who felt they had been disgracefully let down, were all disgusted with the army; and emerging from the first distress began to voice their outrage and despair with little knowledge of the causes of defeat. The Queen would not have this. In a way she had more cause to feel disgraced than anybody else. From first to last she was never heard to say a word against the troops.

Princess Helena Victoria, the sister of Marie Louise, happened to be sitting with the Queen when, pale and shaking, she was examining the casualty list after the appalling defeat at Colenso Hill. The Queen had not said a word. Then she looked up, almost with a toss of the head, and spoke in a firm tone:

'Thora – tell them in the Secretary's office to clear the lines. I want to telegraph to the troops.'

Presently, the Princess returned to the Queen, looking somewhat uneasy.

'Grandmama,' she said, 'they say that it is only customary for the Sovereign to address the troops if they win a Victory, and—'

Suddenly the Queen sat rigid in her chair. Her voice was a whip-lash.

'—Since when have I not been proud of my troops in success or in defeat! Clear the line!'

There are South African War veterans – a few – who remember those days of wretchedness and disillusion at the front. They recall the change in the demoralized men after the posting up of the Queen's telegram.

Lord Esher recalls attending a Queen's Dinner in December 1899. Things were still very bad at the front. A telegram from South Africa was brought in and handed to the Queen at the table. He watched her face turn pale. She held it in a shaking hand as if afraid to tear it open. At last she did so. Somebody rose and read it to her in a whisper. He saw her face relax. This was evidently not a bad one. With a sigh of relief she looked up with a bitter smile and remarked, 'The telegrams from the front make me ill.'

Early in 1900 the Queen was disturbed by family troubles. The matter concerned her favourite granddaughter, Princess Marie Louise, who had married the hereditary Prince of Anhalt, and the crisis occurred so unexpectedly that it must have been a great shock to her grandmother. By the standards of those days it appeared to have the makings of the worst scandal in royal circles for years.

Marie Louise had been the last victim of the old royal custom of *arranged* marriages. She was married off when very young to the heir of the smallest and most hide-bound of German principalities. From the outset she had had nothing in common with her husband. The absurdities of the little Court had filled her with contempt and boredom. There had been no children. Her husband's neglect had suited her very well. She had travelled about the Continent, kept a flat in Berlin, and they rarely saw one another, but the break between them was not widely known.

In 1900, Marie Louise left Germany for a health trip to U.S.A. and Canada, and in her absence her father-in-law the Duke of Anhalt, who had never done anything to help the wedded pair in their difficulties, made a decision. He no longer wanted Marie Louise in the family. His intention, presumably, was to summon her back to Anhalt and then dismiss her for good. The first that Marie Louise knew of all this was when Lord Minto, the Governor-General of Canada, came to her with a telegram from her father-in-law. It ordered her to return to Anhalt immediately. The wording was so sharp that it was plain it bore some sinister meaning; but she was completely at a loss. She was moreover deeply distressed. The telegram had come in *clear*, and many people must know its contents both in Germany and in Canada.

The intention of the Duke of Anhalt had also become known to Queen Victoria through her many German contacts. She perceived the plight of Marie Louise – turned out of Anhalt to wander Europe and with no good reasons offered for her dismissal by the Anhalt family, her favourite granddaughter might be driven into becoming one of those shabby twilight princesses who lurk in the company of seedy adventuresses in the Continental spas and resorts.

An hour after Marie Louise had been handed the telegram from the Duke of Anhalt, Lord Minto came to her again. He held a decoded telegram from Queen Victoria.

'*Tell my granddaughter to come home to me. V.R.*'

Marie Louise never saw Anhalt again, and from that time till the end was frequently the guest of her grandmother.

In the Spring of 1900 the Queen had announced her plan to visit Italy for her holiday. But everybody, including her own family, thought it most injudicious to go abroad, not only because of the danger but because of the still serious war crisis, which was disturbing the country.

As of old, the Queen seemed determined to defy them all and go. She was fully aware of the strong feelings her action would arouse. Lord Esher notes, as Henry Ponsonby had done before him that, 'nobody dare tackle *H.M.*!'

When it became known what she was going to do, the sensation and indeed the dismay was much stronger than if she had gone to the Continent. She was going to go to Ireland. The Irish themselves were struck dumb by the news. She had not been seen in Ireland for half a century. The Irish had been dangerous hosts for English Sovereigns even in those distant days, and they were considered to be far more so in 1900, for the indignation against the Queen for outspokenly opposing Home Rule had been very fierce, and there were plenty of patriots who had uttered murderous threats against her.

The Queen announced that she was coming to Ireland in special recognition of the most gallant services of her Irish regiments in South Africa. It was a reason likely to touch the hearts of the sentimental Irish; but nevertheless everybody knew that there were grim risks involved. Even if the visit did not end tragically, it might well turn out a dismal and humiliating failure.

In actuality, the Irish visit, which covered several weeks, was a wonderful triumph for the aged Queen. The sight of her was too much for the Irish. She carried them with her completely. It must have been a strange experience to some veterans in her suite, who could recall the grim days of the seventies. The Queen was obviously revelling in her Irish visit.

It would perhaps be inaccurate to suggest that the strain of the Irish visit killed the Queen; but it was her last 'holiday' beyond seas, and after that, few of those about her believed that she had long to live, although they could not imagine her actually dying.

She suffered from no noticeable complaint, and outsiders, such as generals who came from the front and were invited to visit her at Windsor were deeply impressed and declared themselves inspired by her vigour, courage and startling understanding of their problems. She talked as if she was contemplating going to South Africa herself, and had she been younger when such disasters befell the troops it seemed highly probable that whatever advice was given her she would have done so.

In December 1900 she was very far from well, and the doctors were expressing some anxiety. She was frequently absent from her dinner-table, which was always a bad sign. But she insisted that the officers of a Canadian Light Horse regiment should dine with her at Windsor.

Her Canadian guests had no idea that she was failing, and were entranced by her lively manner. Lord Esher tells us that the regimental adjutant was so moved that after bidding her good-bye he murmured tearfully, 'I could die for Her!'

It was on 16 January 1901, that the Queen first became seriously ill. Next day Sir Douglas Powell, the lung and heart specialist, arrived at Osborne. He decided to stay overnight and suggested that the Prince of Wales and the members of the family should be called.

On the nineteenth, when carriage after carriage bringing royalty were drawing up at the door and a busy hush prevailed in the rapidly filling house, the news went round that the Queen was much better. But the physicians were not optimistic, and the first public bulletin was put out to warn the Empire of what might be expected at any time.

In the meanwhile the German Emperor was known to be on his way, and the overflowing population of Osborne burst out in expressions of violent indignation. They seemed to have no objection to the suite and the servants overhearing their opinions about the Kaiser, so that there could be no doubt the German Embassy would report everything to Berlin. The Prince of Wales, who could never forgive the Kaiser for nicknaming him 'the old popinjay', and who might expect to become King at any time, preserved no restraint on the subject of this hateful nephew to whom he must shortly be a brother sovereign. A telegram was sent to meet the Kaiser in London. It advised him to stay there. His presence was not required at Osborne. The Prince himself returned to Marlborough House.

On the evening of the twenty-first the Prince of Wales was again summoned to Osborne, and the Kaiser also took train for the Isle of Wight. On the morning of the twenty-second there could be little doubt that the end was near.

When the Prince of Wales came to the Queen in the morning there was a dazed look in her eyes. Presently they lit up. She had recognized him, and she put out her hand, murmuring, 'Bertie'.

Perhaps he had not heard her use such soft tones to him for more than half a century. He broke down.

Shortly afterwards the Queen's old friend the Bishop of Ripon entered the bedroom and approaching the bed knelt down and began to pray. The Queen certainly knew who he was: her face relaxed and she almost smiled. But she watched him in silence and after a considerable period of prayer she let him rise and leave her in silence. No sooner was he gone than she stirred and said in quite a firm voice, 'I think I ought to see Canon Clement-Smith (the Vicar of Whippenham) – otherwise he will be hurt.'

Early that afternoon the Queen's bedroom was full of people. All of those who should be there had been called. They were waiting for the end.

Nobody could say how it came about that while the Prince of Wales stood in a great state of distress at the foot of his mother's bed, the Queen died in the arms of the German Emperor – that wickedest grandson for whom she always had a soft spot and who in his strange childish way loved her perhaps better than any of them. But so it turned out. They were both enigmas, apart from other people, and may have had something in common.

It may have happened because the Queen was then fighting for life and when she wanted help people had turned their eyes from the painful spectacle. Suddenly the Kaiser had been seen kneeling by the pillow, supporting her with his arm while Dr Reid did the same on the other side of the bed. The two men with limbs and faces set like statues knelt for a long time as the Queen rallied and failed and rallied again. Sometimes her wild gaze lit upon someone in the room and she gasped out their names, always correctly. They took to calling out their names to her one by one in pleading voices. It was dramatic and it was horrible.

The Duke of Argyll, then Lord-in-Waiting was watching the struggle, and afterwards he likened it to 'the sinking of a great three-decker ship'.

Even the aftermath of the death of this strangest of Queens was unexpected. It was the German Emperor – not one of her own children – who took charge of everything in an utterly bewildered Court. It was he, not an undertaker, who measured the Queen for her coffin, and he who later summoned the Duke of Connaught to help him and Dr Reid lift the corpse into the coffin.

A further touch of drama befitting the subject came with the discovery of the Marochetti effigy. In mid-century, Marochetti, the celebrated Italian sculptor, had executed a recumbent marble figure of the Queen. The figure had been forgotten for years until the Queen, a few months before her death, told Lord Esher that it was somewhere at Windsor. She wanted it above her tomb. He thought the matter could rest till the Queen actually died. After her death he asked the Clerk of the Works at the Castle to produce the statue. He had never heard of it. Nor, apparently, had anybody else. They searched the Castle from end to end. Esher was baffled, and the family hearing of the Queen's wish was growing agitated.

Then an aged workman suddenly recalled a day's work in the sixties. He had helped brick up the entrance of a storeroom stacked with Castle rubbish in 1865. The man believed he had seen a white statue lying in the gloom. He led them to the bare brick wall, the entrance was unbricked and there, covered in dirt, was the Queen's effigy. Esher had it placed on top of the Tomb in the Royal Mausoleum at Frogmore.

Two further items of fantasy marked the Queen's passing: both of these might have stirred a chortle in the heroine of the brown roans' adventure could she have witnessed them.

On her last journey to the mainland, clumsiness all but sent her coffin diving into the Solent.

At Windsor the icy hill outside the station was too much for the team of horses of the Royal Horse Artillery. They slid, kicked and bucked, entangling the traces, and the little bedecked coffin danced and rocked, watched by its horrified attendants.

A sudden order, given just in time, saved a macabre disaster. The sailors lining the route ran forward and cut the tangled traces with their jack-knives. The gunners with murder in their eyes hovered in ill-restrained fury, as the sailors, ignoring their tight-lipped menace, improvised drag ropes and set off to pull the royal guncarriage up to the Castle. It was a unique gesture to a unique Queen, re-enacted each time a British sovereign dies.

Bibliography

SOME WORKS CONSULTED

Queen Victoria by Lytton Strachey
Queen Victoria by H. & A. Gersheim
Daughters of Queen Victoria by E. F. Benson
Albert the Good by Hector Bolitho
The Prince Consort & His Brother: Letters by Hector Bolitho
Recollections of Three Reigns by Sir Frederick Ponsonby
Under Six Reigns by Princess Marie-Louise
King Edward VII (2 vols.) by Sir Sidney Lee
H.R.H. Princess Mary Adelaide of Teck (2 vols.) by C. Kinloch Cooke
The Day I Knew by Lily Langtry
Life of Tennyson by Hallam Tennyson
The Shy Princess (H.R.H. Princess Beatrice) by Douglas Duff
Queen Victoria at Windsor & Balmoral by Princess Victoria of Prussia
    (edit. J. Pope-Hennessy)
A Distant Summer by Edith Saunders
Henry Irving by Laurence Irving
Story of My Life by Ellen Terry
As We Were by E. F. Benson
Henry Ponsonby—his life from his letters by Arthur Ponsonby
Letters of Queen Victoria
Letters of Empress Frederick of Prussia
Letters of Lady Augusta Stanley
Letters & Journal Lady Mary Ponsonby
Diary and Correspondence of H. Wellesley, Lord Cowley
Journals and Letters of Viscount Esher (2 vols.)
Creevey Papers

Index

ATE